Tobago

An Introduction and Guide

Eaulin Blondel

MACMILLAN
CARIBBEAN

Macmillan Education
Between Towns Road, Oxford OX4 3PP
A division of Macmillan Publishers Limited
Companies and representatives throughout the world

www.macmillan-caribbean.com

ISBN 0 333 91407 4

Typeset by CjB Editorial Plus
Illustrated by TechType
Cover design by Gary Fielder, AC Design
Cover photographs by Donald Nausbaum

The authors and publishers would like to thank the following
for permission to reproduce their material:
Environment Tobago (pages 102–103); Kariwak Village Hotel
(pages 45, 50).

Printed and bound in Malaysia

2007 2006 2005 2004 2003
10 9 8 7 6 5 4 3 2 1

Contents

Acknowledgements   v

Welcome to Tobago   vi

Part I – The island

1   The island of Tobago   3
2   A history of Tobago   17

Part II – The people of the island

3   True, true Tobagonian   33
4   Food – Tobago-style   43
5   Politics and government   52
6   Festivals and celebrations   60
7   Sporting grounds   71
8   Tobago's art scene   79

Part III – The environment

9   Eco-Tobago   89
10   Exploring inland waters: waterfalls and river walks   104
11   Agriculture   111
12   Off the deep end in Tobago   121

Part IV – Touring the island

13   The Caribbean coast: Crown Point to Arnos Vale   135
14   The Northside Road   157
15   Scarborough   167
16   The Windward Road   179
17   Additional information   192

Acknowledgements

Always one needs help. I have been extremely fortunate while writing this guide to have had the assistance of good friends who wanted, as much as I did, to have it done right.

First of all there's Dr Pamela Collins of Tobago, an agriculturist with other keen interests as well, who provided me with all of the information for the chapter on agriculture and read large portions of the entire script of the book for accuracy of content.

Dr Bridget Brereton, Deputy Principal and Professor of History at the University of the West Indies, St Augustine, Trinidad, was kind enough to let me impose on our friendship by asking her to vet the history chapters related to the Amerindians and to Europe in Tobago. I benefited greatly from her suggestions and advice.

Mr Edward Hernandez, Curator of the Tobago Museum, Fort King George, Scarborough, generously and efficiently cleared up many a knotty problem for me over the course of writing the book.

Mark Puddy, an adventurous Englishman in Scarborough, friend and popular tour escort with an intimate knowledge of Tobago's inland waters, was very kind to supply me with most of the information on rivers and waterfalls.

Jean Pearse of Tobago, friend of my childhood, has been my hostess on many a trip to Tobago seeking out information. She has been kind, thoughtful and totally accommodating and tolerant.

Then of course there's Nicholas Gillard of Macmillan, who first said 'yes, do it' and then went on to be absolutely supportive and very kind.

Thank you folks!

Eaulin Blondel

Welcome to Tobago

Welcome to Tobago - where beauty is in the eye of the beholder all day long, where the pulse quickens at the richness of green mountains and pleasant pastures, the incredible turquoise of the sea and the startling blue of a blue-gray tanager on the wing.

Tobago is the fulfilment of a dream. It is the reality that was waiting for those adventurers of old, the pot of gold at the end of their rainbow. Today, you will find a visit here a delightful experience. Time and nature have combined to make the island beautiful, exciting and romantic.

Many nations have fought to maintain their supremacy in Tobago and each, in some way, left its mark on how we are now. Some of our music and dance, for example the reel and the jig, were inherited from the British; many of our villages carry the names of towns in the distant lands from which their original owners came - Pembroke, Speyside, Glamorgan, Runnemede; some again are reminders of the various groups which Tobago attracted, including those swashbuckling buccaneers - Man O' War Bay, Pirates' Bay, and Louis d'Or. Names such as Pigeon Point, Turtle Beach (where turtles still visit) and Parrot Hall all attest to the richness of our animal life. All of these are reminders of who we are, of what we have experienced, of what the land knows in its secret self.

And then there are the things we do. We have fishermen's festivals and harvest festivals. Almost every week in Tobago there is a village harvest, when one village plays host to the rest of Tobago, inviting everyone to visit, to enjoy the church service and the evening cantata by the choir, to eat, drink and be merry. In July the Heritage Festival takes you down the history road back to old times, reliving Tobago's past - its heritage - through village-related activity: two weeks of song, dance and drama, beautiful costuming, fun and laughter that were all part of old-time Tobago.

These are some of the treasures that we offer, for we have the usual, the unusual and the startlingly different - like motmots, beautiful birds with such an appetite for cheese that they will take it from your open palm.

Aerial view of Pigeon Point (MIKE TOY)

We have glorious sunsets and beautiful moonlight nights. We have sand - glistening white sand, black sand! Did anyone mention the sun warming your back, breezes blowing softly against your cheek? What about the beaches? Did we mention lying in the shade of a tree listening to the ocean? Or cool coconut water, straight from the nut, or steel band music wafting on the wind? In Tobago? YES!!

Approaching Buccoo Reef *following page* (MIKE TOY)

| PART I |

The island

| 1 |

The island of Tobago

Eleven Degrees North is the name of one of Tobago's excellent restaurants. Plus 15 minutes, it represents this island's distance north of the Equator, with 60 degrees and 40 minutes west longitude.

Lying 21 miles (34 km) north-east of Trinidad, its sister isle in the Republic of Trinidad and Tobago, Tobago forms the final link in that chain of mountain ranges which extends eastwards from the Venezuelan coastal range in South America. Being on the extreme edge of the continental shelf, a comparatively shallow passage of water separates it from Trinidad, but very deep waters indeed divide it from its closest neighbours, Grenada and Barbados.

Though washed by both the Atlantic Ocean and the Caribbean Sea, Tobago is more closely related geologically to the South American mainland than it is to the other islands of the Caribbean to the north. It's a small island, only 116 square miles (300 sq km) in area, being 21 miles long (34 km) and only seven and a half miles (12 km) broad at its widest point.

Its major topographical feature is a central spine of forest-clad hard rock known as the Main Ridge, which, starting in the north-east, stretches along the northern part of the island, reaching a height of 1860 feet (549 m), with no well-defined peak but with steep ridges and gullies, until the land eventually flattens out to the south-west into low-lying land of coral formation which has been called Lowlands.

Tobago's climate is, in a nutshell, long hours of sunshine and cooling sea breezes, resembling that of the Lesser Antilles more than that of Trinidad. The prevailing winds are the north-east trades which, coming in and rising over the high mountain ridges of the eastern portion of the island, bring a significantly higher rainfall to this area than occurs in the west of the island, and lower humidity generally than that experienced in Trinidad. The average daytime temperature is 29°C (83°F), with nights being cooler – not chilly, just cooler.

There are none of the dramatic changes in climate of the island that give temperate countries so much variety in a year. There are just two

Pigeon Point *opposite* (MIKE TOY)

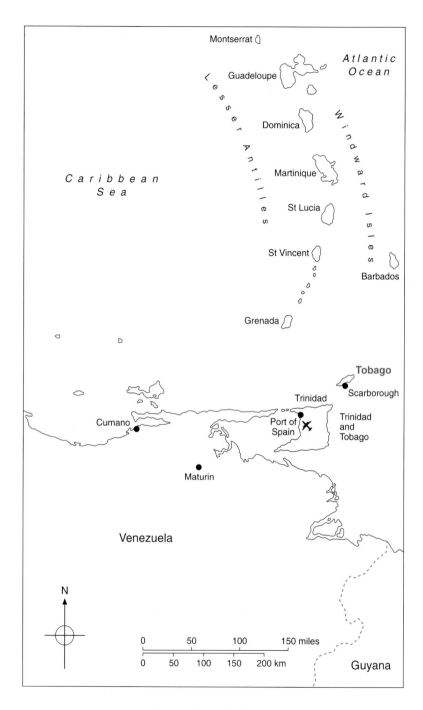

The southern Caribbean

4

**Barbados Bay and Granby Point from the Windward Road,
near Mount St George** (MICHAEL BOURNE)

seasons - the dry and the wet (also known as 'rainy') - but the tenor
of lives and behaviour patterns of the people are affected by these two
seasons just as much as the lives of those who experience four seasons
are affected by spring, summer, autumn and winter.

December to May marks the dry season and June to December, the
rainy. The divisions are not rigid however, and sometimes everything
seems to go absolutely haywire, with too much of one season
occurring in the other - for example, too long a dry spell in the rainy
season or vice versa - but generally speaking it goes the way it should
and one can plan activities to suit.

A road near Plymouth (MIKE TOY)

Blue skies are the order of the day in the dry season. Blue skies, a hot, untiring sun and high winds. The early part of the dry season is the windiest time of the year, and locals take advantage of the high breezes by indulging in kite flying, particularly around Christmas time, when 'mad bulls', 'chikki chongs' and other popular types of kites made of coloured paper and cocoyea taken from the fronds of the coconut palm, take to the sky. Tobagonian youngsters do a brisk trade with kites of all shapes and colours at this time.

The rainy or wet season lives up to its name, but thankfully it is wet rather than cold, and although skies are often overcast, the sun is

frequently out, bringing enough breaks in the weather to make a vacation at this time enjoyable. Locals make the most of these breaks in the weather. They need the rain and want it, so they manage day-time rain with raised eyebrows, umbrellas and a grumble, but enjoy the rain at night, pounding on the rooftops. It's the greatest lullaby you can experience and one of the pluses of tropical-island living, where extra storeys don't get in the way between you and the rooftop.

Tucked away in the rainy season, however, is a time for caution, and there's a rhyme that says:

> *June too soon.*
> *July stand by.*
> *August come it must,*
> *September, remember,*
> *October all over.*

This is the hurricane rhyme. Trinidad and Tobago lie outside the hurricane belt, but occasional storms occur. Most of these are not particularly violent, but in 1963 a hurricane named Flora devastated Tobago, causing widespread damage to property and crops and seriously affecting the natural environment: so much of the natural vegetation was destroyed that there was a notable change in the quantity of wildlife, particularly birds, and some species disappeared completely for a very long time. However, Nature has been putting in regenerative growth, and gradually the situation improves.

The origin of the hurricane rhyme is unknown, but many believe that it is an old mariners' rhyme, invented by Caribbean sailors of long ago to remind them of tricky weather time in the Caribbean Sea.

Azure waters at Pigeon Point *following pages* (MIKE TOY)

View up the windward coast from Fort King George (MIKE TOY)

Another feature of the rainy season is the Petite Careme, which is a short, dry spell of about seven to 14 days, occurring in the rainy season, usually around September to October.

Because so much land has been cleared for agriculture, the natural vegetation of Tobago, that is, the original vegetation, is to be found mainly in the protected Main Ridge Forest Reserve and adjoining Crown lands. Tobago's Main Ridge boasts the oldest legally protected forest reserve of its kind in the hemisphere. It is more than two centuries old and was brought about by the superior ecological understanding engendered in one Soames Jenyns of England by a scientist called Hales, around 1774 or 1775.

Hales explained to Jenyns the relationship between trees and rainfall, thus alerting him to the possible danger for Tobago that lay in the destruction of acres and acres of forested land by planters intent upon growing sugar cane.

Tropical forest pathway on Little Tobago *opposite* (MIKE TOY)

Jenyns, luckily, was at that time one of the Lord's Commissioners of Trade and Plantations, and was responsible for settling Tobago under British rule after 1763. He was therefore in a position to effect change and in 1775 he declared the area known as the Main Ridge Reserve to be Crown Reserve.

Silk cotton tree (MICHAEL BOURNE)

Bamboos near Englishman's Bay (MICHAEL BOURNE)

Of course the planter faction in the British Parliament did not easily accept his proposal, but he managed finally to convince them that the destruction of the forest would result in total denudation of the land, and they eventually yielded to his entreaties. The Ordinance was signed in 1776 by Governor Sir William Young and stated that the land had been reserved to the Crown for 'the purpose of attracting frequent showers of rain upon which fertility of the lands in these climates doth entirely depend'.

So there it is, a tropical rainforest, luxuriant and evergreen. On the Ridge itself there are rosewood and redwood trees, wild coffee and others, stretching from about 800 feet (245 m) above sea level; but in other parts, north and south of the Ridge, one finds cyp and crapaud trees, while on Little Tobago and St Giles islands in the north-east, vegetation is essentially naked indian trees and palms, with shrubs.

Outside the protected area though, there are numerous other trees to be found. The most common of these is the mango in all its varieties, and there are avocado and tamarind trees aplenty with the ubiquitous hog plum and breadfruit trees competing for attention. There are tall, woody, sapodilla trees, hundreds of tall, skinny, umbrella-like papaya trees, and literally thousands of gracefully waving coconut palms, despite the fact that the coconut industry is now almost dead. Tobagonians, in company with West Indian people generally, dearly love the water of the green coconuts – coconut water – and the soft, delicious jelly inside.

Flowering trees are also plentiful, and, especially in the dry season, light the hillsides and perfume the air with their glorious coloured blooms. Of these the golden poui is the most often seen, and

A castor bean plant (MIKE TOY)

Yellow hibiscus (MIKE TOY)

Ashanti blood bush (MIKE TOY)

Heliconia flower (MIKE TOY)

15

positively the most breathtaking in its beauty. It flames on the hillsides and on the plains from around March and sometimes as early as February until the month of May, perhaps even until June when the rains come. There are pink pouis as well, but these are not as common or as striking as the gold. Then again there is the flamboyant tree, a graceful, thick-trunked, wide-spreading tree, which like the poui loses all its leaves and presents an absolutely bare face to the world until suddenly, one day, it bursts into glorious red, yellow or orange blooms, sending the hummingbird population into a feeding frenzy.

Yet another variety of flowering tree is the madre de cocoa, the immortelle, so called because it was originally planted by cocoa estate owners to shade the young cocoa trees from the sun. It's a tall, graceful tree which blooms into orange or red flowers and is particularly prevalent in the eastern areas. The orange-winged parrot absolutely loves the flowers of this tree!

A host of shrubs, herbs and flowering plants make up the rest of Tobago's vegetation and are regularly found in home gardens, because Tobagonians have a fondness for what they often refer to as 'flowers'.

Perhaps the most common plant is the bougainvillea, but then almost as prolific are the hibiscus in all its varieties, the yellow and purple allamanda, rose bushes and the dwarf poinciana or pride of Barbados, which is also a hummingbird favourite. Have a tree in your garden and you'll see them constantly!

| 2 |
A history of Tobago

Amerindians and the first settlers

In the early days, long before the arrival of Columbus in the western hemisphere, Tobago, like every other Caribbean island, had her share of Amerindian tenants. It has not been possible to pinpoint exactly who they all were, but archaeologists and historians consider them to have been Caribs and Arawaks. It seems that the Caribs, being a warlike, aggressive race, steadfastly drove all the weaker tribes before them, constantly attacking. Where they came from no one knows exactly, but it is thought that they were part of a great migration from the area between the Amazon and Orinoco rivers in the continent of South America, many, many years before 1498. They and the Arawaks are considered to have been Stone Age peoples.

The Arawaks were the native peoples of the Greater Antilles. Before Spanish expansion in the Caribbean their numbers had been considerably reduced because of constant war with the Caribs and also because of interbreeding, but there were still some Arawaks in Tobago and many in Trinidad at the time of Columbus's sighting.

The arrival of Spain found the Caribs still very active in the Caribbean, raiding, burning, capturing and killing the island Arawaks. The Caribs' violent antipathy to Europeans was immediate upon contact but it is important to remember in their favour that their opposition to the establishment of all European settlements was in defence of their homeland.

They frequently attacked Spanish landing parties, killing many and taking prisoners whom they used as slave labour. This caused the Spaniards, who were themselves intent upon claiming territory and plundering, a great deal of annoyance and discomfort. There is much written in histories about the evidence of Carib cannibalism that the Spaniards claimed to have witnessed.

Eventually in 1511, the King of Spain was compelled to issue a *cedula* - a type of royal decree - which would adversely affect the whole Indian population in the Caribbean, not just the Caribs, although it was primarily directed against them. This *cedula* permitted all persons to wage war against the Caribs in the King's name and kill them or sell them into slavery; it opened the way for the enslavement and destruction of all Indians who offered any resistance whatever, for who could tell one Indian from another, Carib from Arawak?

In the end, therefore, despite the belligerent Caribs, the Europeans were too formidable an opponent and their weaponry was far superior to bows and arrows. The warlike Caribs were vanquished and virtually wiped out. Many committed suicide, their indomitable spirit choosing death in favour of captivity. Only a few hundred of them still exist today in Dominica, St Vincent and the Guyana region, as well as in Central America where some 'Black Caribs' survive.

At the time when Columbus saw her in the distance and named her Assumption, Tobago had already been named Tabaco by the Caribs, because of her long, slender, pipe-like shape, resembling the long-stemmed pipe they used for smoking. The English word for tabaco is tobacco. It is thought that the Indians first used tobacco as a narcotic drink and for ceremonial purposes, since they believed it to have medicinal qualities.

Artefacts in the museums in Tobago and Trinidad are practically all that remains of those early Tobagonians, but it is still possible to find shards of pottery on the seashore, particularly in places like Grand Courland and Plymouth, where native tribes are known to have resided. These artefacts provide indisputable evidence of the Amerindian presence in early Tobago, and even today digging continues. A group of youngsters from France and their tutor, Leonid Kamenoff, on an archaeological expedition known as the Jules Verne Expedition on the ship *Karrek Ven*, have been studying Amerindian cultures of the Orinoco past and present, and have visited Tobago for several years to conduct archaeological digs. One of their discoveries has been a human skeleton found in Courland Bay, which has been carbon dated as being 800 years old.

Amerindian refuse heaps that have been unearthed remind us that warfare apart, the way of life of these people was very simple. They made their own pottery as well as their bows and arrows, dipping the points of the arrows in the juice from the fruit of the manchineel tree, which is highly poisonous.

Food was plentiful and easily accessible. They cultivated cassava or manioc and a wide variety of fruits. There were deer, armadillo, wild hog, manicou and iguana for which traps were set, and there were also highly edible birds such as the cocrico – the Tobago pheasant; this bird is still numerous on the island today, because it is the national bird of Tobago and protected.

The yield from the sea was every bit as generous, for fi[s] abundant and fields of whelks, conchs and other shellfish the sea rocks. Turtles also came to the beaches as they sti[ll] lay large numbers of eggs, which have always been consi[dered a] great delicacy. The depredations of these native peoples upon the turtle population were not nearly as terrible as those of twentieth-century man have been.

Europe and Tobago

The truly significant period of Tobago's history really starts in the eighteenth century, after British rule was established. The institutions and developments introduced by Britain laid the foundations of the Tobago that exists today.

However, the seventeenth century was a very colourful and dramatic period for Tobago. No permanent political change occurred, but there was plenty of swashbuckling valour and adventure. Tobago was like a shuttlecock, batted back and forth between the settlers from different countries, with the ever-warring Caribs and local conditions such as fever and disease acting as very effective delimiters as far as the growth of settlements was concerned.

The main contenders in the wrangling over Tobago between the fifteenth and eighteenth centuries were the Dutch, the Courlanders (from Latvia), the French and the English. These were the European nations that suffered the greatest losses in the Tobago enterprise. Intent upon expansion, new dominion and trade, they saw Tobago as a prize which none would permit the others to gain or keep.

For much of this period Europe was at war, and this war was brought into the Caribbean by its contenders, France, Holland, England and Spain. Tobago was part of the Caribbean extension of the feud to the extent that if a Dutch settlement was built and discovered, then the French or the English would destroy it and vice versa.

Then there were the Courlanders, who made Tobago a target of colonising zeal in their scramble to gain overseas colonies. Holland and Courland, though not at war with one another, each made repeatedly determined attempts to establish large settlements in Tobago.

Under the power of a Grant from Charles I of England, the Courlanders set their minds and hearts upon Tobago and made no

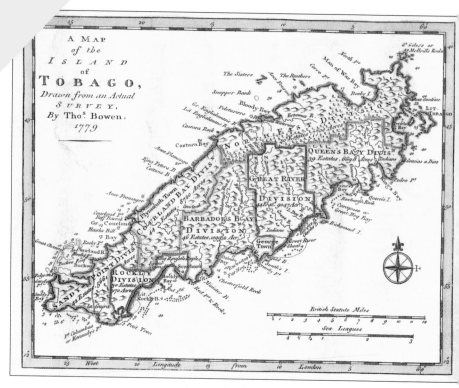

A map of Tobago in 1779

fewer than three determined attempts to establish large settlements, first with an expedition of about 200 men in 1639, then again in 1642 with 310 men, and in 1654 with 80 families, 125 soldiers and 25 officers, all at Jacobus Bay (Great Courland). While many of these settlements were successful for a period of time, destruction always overtook them eventually and Tobago was for much of the time deserted, particularly after the Caribs had begun to die out.

Spain seems to have had no interest whatsoever in Tobago and definitely made no attempt to settle it. In 1614 Johannes Roderigo, a Spaniard, had attempted to establish trade with the Caribs of Tobago, but after a four-month stay in the island, finding the Indians too numerous and unwelcoming, he had despaired and returned to Trinidad.

Essentially, the Spaniards were intent upon their search for El Dorado, the City of Gold. But Tobago's nearness to Trinidad, where they had established themselves in the late sixteenth century, made them wary. Their hold in Trinidad was very tenuous and the Indians (Nepuyos)

The Courland Monument (MICHAEL BOURNE)

constantly harassed them. So in November 1636, when they learned that the Dutch had built two forts in Tobago, had also been ambitious enough to establish a small trading post at Point Galera (the north-eastern corner of Trinidad) and were actually friendly with the Nepuyos in that area, they became alarmed, fearing the result of an Indian–Dutch alliance.

Diego Lopez de Escobar, then Governor of Trinidad, decided to attack first. In August 1636 the Spaniards destroyed the smaller Dutch fort in Rockly Bay and took prisoners. But apart from this concern with their own security, the Spaniards left Tobago alone.

The Dutch, it seems, were as persevering and determined as the Courlanders, but they had no more fortune than the Courlanders in Tobago. They did manage to establish a very large settlement at Roodklyp Bay, which was in the area of present-day Rockly Bay in the town of Scarborough. They built a fort - Dutch Fort - just facing the present Scarborough port, and developed plantations and sugar works, constructed a Great House, bought numerous slaves and servants, cattle and horses, and built a thriving community. It seemed that Holland had come into her own in Tobago after 40 years and was at last receiving her reward. But the inevitable happened in 1665, when British privateers under agreement with the Governor of Jamaica destroyed the settlement.

One of the greatest battles that took place in Tobago was fought in 1677 between the Dutch, who were again in occupancy of the island, and the French, who were seeking revenge for the depredations of the Dutch upon their colonies in Marie Galante and Cayenne. The French managed to sail their ships directly into Roodklyp Bay, and at close range set on fire many Dutch ships. It was a terrific battle, lasting seven

Sign commemorating the site of a seventeenth-century Dutch-Courlander fortification (MICHAEL BOURNE)

hours. Of the 14 French ships engaged, only seven were able to come out of Roodklyp Bay. French losses amounted to 1200 killed and wounded. The Dutch lost half of their total crew of 800 men and their entire fleet, and would lose the remainder when the French returned to finish the job in December 1677 and literally blew the fort into the sky!

For several years after this Dutch defeat by the French in Roodklyp Bay, repeated attempts were made by England, Holland, France and Courland (again) to establish themselves in Tobago. Meanwhile marauding pirates had got in on the act, making the island a base for their attacks upon shipping in the area. The British dispelled the pirates and now being in earnest about their claim to Tobago, refused all petitions made to them to settle the island, although they themselves

The conquest of Tobago by England, 1703 (PARIA PUBLISHING CO. LTD)

did not settle it. Tobago had become a sort of no-man's land, until around 1705 a French squadron started using it as a base for attacking other English West Indian islands and carried out raids all over the Southern Caribbean.

By 1714 the many changes of settlers in Tobago had left a number of blacks free on the island, and it is interesting to note that in that year the head Indian Chief of Tobago appealed to the Governor of Barbados for protection against them. The Governor assured the Chief of protection and by so doing reinforced Britain's claim to sole sovereignty of the island. However, in 1725 Barbados, in response to an order to establish a settlement in Tobago, advised the British Government that until France and Britain could settle matters between them, it would be pointless to try starting any English settlement in Tobago only to have it destroyed by the French. Barbadian settlers were unwilling to risk such a venture.

1748 saw the French from Martinique landing troops in Tobago and building a fort, but the British complained to the French Government, who disowned the act, and both governments agreed to declare the island neutral. Subjects of both nations left the island and the fort was destroyed. But it was not long before the French had re-established their settlement.

Fourteen years later, in 1762, the English recaptured Tobago, and the Treaty of Paris ceded it to Britain in 1763.

Building a country

Britain's claim to Tobago having been guaranteed by the Treaty of Paris, the British Government proceeded to include Tobago in its plan for colonisation of the Windward Islands, whereby the island was put with Grenada, St Vincent and Dominica under a Governor-in-Chief, whose residence was in Grenada. The first Lieutenant Governor of Tobago, Alexander Brown, arrived on the island on 12 November 1764.

Now that the defence of the island was secure for the first time in more than 200 years, settlers from Europe and other West Indian Islands began arriving in large numbers bringing their slaves, personal property and a good deal of capital for investment.

Much land was available and one of Alexander Brown's earliest acts as Governor was to issue a proclamation concerning that land. Tobago was to be divided into seven parishes, and roads were to be mapped out. Land for sale was offered on very attractive terms, so that it was possible to acquire 500 acres of virgin land for the small deposit of £100, with the balance to be paid in five yearly instalments. In the interests of security a belt of land three chains (198 feet) in width next to the sea coast was reserved for the building of forts and defences. Approximately 54 400 acres of land were sold under this proclamation. The first record of purchase is in the name of James Simpson for lot No. 1 at Courland Bay.

Georgetown, near modern-day Studley Park at Barbados Bay, was the first town established. It was intended to be the seat of government and the first meeting of the Legislative Council was held there, but its administrative importance did not last because it was felt to be unhealthy, being too near to a swamp (part of which is still there), and the capital was moved to Scarborough. The fort built to defend Georgetown had been called Granby Fort. The name remains, as indeed does one lone grave, but all the fortifications were removed and sent to Fort King George in Scarborough. Nevertheless, Granby does have some claim to fame as the place from which the first shipment of sugar

Sign at Fort Milford (MICHAEL BOURNE)

produced by the British on Studley Park Estate was shipped; it was loaded onto the *Dolly* in 1770.

Progress had come to Tobago. Every aspect of her development was being planned. Law and government, business, population growth – all of these were coming together. Sugar was, of course, the principal crop and with good reason. Prices on the British market were high and the island itself was ideally suited to its production.

So impressive was the development that in 1768 the Secretary of State gave his permission for Tobago to have a colonial legislature. A General Council consisting only of planters was appointed by an Order in Council on 12 February 1768 and a council chamber was built and in use by April of the same year. Not too long after that the Legislature of Tobago came into being, with an upper house consisting of appointed members and a lower house of elected members. Qualifications for voting were to be male, Christian and British, 21 years old and with an annual income of £20. In order to stand for elections one had to be Protestant, male, British, 21 years old and owner of 50 acres of land or a town property that would earn £50 per year.

But all was not well in paradise. From 1764 onwards there had been large imports of slaves to supply the demands of the plantations. In 1770 there was a slave revolt at Queen's Bay. A now-famous slave named Sandy and his followers, wanting to be free men, rose up in violence against those who held them in bondage. However, the uprising failed. Sandy had not been able to recruit as many to his cause as he had hoped. Some of his group, women included, were taken, tortured and hanged, as a deterrent to future insurrectionists. Sandy himself is believed to have fled to Trinidad. The lesson, however, was not at all well learned by the slaves for there were two more uprisings in 1771 and 1774, which were speedily put down by the militia.

Slave revolts apart, Tobago must have been in this period of rapid plantation development a highly invigorating place for those engaged in her growth. From being a more or less deserted island steadfastly repelling settlers, she had become a place of industry, powered by slavery. By 1775 her population had mushroomed to 2300 whites, 1050 free coloured and 10 800 slaves. There were sugar cane and cotton estates, windmills to power the needed water and 'great houses' for owners of the estates and their families.

Fort Milford *opposite* (MICHAEL BOURNE)

But Nature had her own little adjustments to make. In 1775 disaster struck in the form of a plague of ants which destroyed sugar cane plantations from the windward coast right across the island. Sugar had to be abandoned as a staple in favour of cotton, and much capital was lost.

Then the Americans entered the scene. In 1777, with the British-American war in progress, American privateers arrived in armed boats and raided the island, escaping with what they could in a hit and run exercise. In 1778, an American squadron of two ships, three brigs and a schooner were on their way to capture Tobago when they ran into the British 60-gunner *Yarmouth* which put an end to their ambitions. But Britain, having had to deploy ships and troops to the American conflict, was weak in the Caribbean. France, having joined the American War against Britain, perceived this weakness and took Grenada in 1779. In April 1781 French ships advanced upon Tobago, captured the island and took the Governor prisoner.

Tobago was catapulted into her French experience – a 12-year period of French rule. It does not seem to have been an unbearable time for the British in Tobago, for the French did not change either the Constitution or laws which had been established under British rule, and plantation development continued between 1781 and 1793. Two major events of the period were the revolt among French troops in which Scarborough was burned down and the hurricane of 1790, which brought widespread destruction.

On 15 April 1793, at the start of the Revolutionary War, the British recaptured Tobago, re-established the legal and political set-up of 1768 and made the island entirely independent of any other West Indian colony. But the Treaty of Amiens in 1802 gave Tobago to the French, who again refrained from making administrative changes. This was just as well, for by 1803 war had again erupted between France and Britain and a British naval force invaded Tobago, putting it right back into British hands for good this time, although it was not until 1814 that the Treaty of Paris ratified this.

The slave trade was abolished in all British dominions in 1807 and this carried serious labour implications for places like Tobago which were dependent upon slave labour. However Tobago, unlike Trinidad, already had a large slave population by this time and so would not have felt the cessation of the Trade so keenly.

Emancipation and the apprenticeship system came into force in 1834 and even though Tobago shared in the rejoicing that took place

The conquest of Tobago by France (PARIA PUBLISHING CO. LTD)

throughout the British West Indies, the outlook from the planters' view-point was not so good, because when freedom was granted to all apprentices in 1838, a shortage of labour due to the planters' inability to pay the ex-slaves a wage brought many difficulties. The land was not being worked efficiently. Crops were poor, agriculture was in a bad state and many estates went out of cultivation.

Despite the problems, the infrastructure of the island kept developing. Schools were founded, the West Indies Bank opened in Scarborough, churches of different denominations opened their doors and the Royal Mail Steam Packet Company began calling at Tobago. In 1843 one Mr Cruickshank, in an effort to improve agriculture, introduced the Metayer system – a profit-sharing arrangement which was eventually adopted throughout the country.

By 1851 the population had soared to 14 378 and was further augmented on two separate occasions by liberated Africans from St Helena who were brought in by the British Government to ease the labour shortage.

The police force was strengthened in 1854, but then Britain withdrew her troops from Fort King George and the inhabitants had to make their own arrangements to preserve law and order.

From the economic viewpoint, the situation was not good. The sugar industry was declining steadily and exports of by-products were in serious decline. The Belmanna Riots occurred in the Windward districts in 1876, and in 1884 the British firm which virtually owned the sugar business in Tobago, having a monopoly on agriculture and shipping and owning four-fifths of the sugar estates, stopped the payment of bills to planters. This was disastrous; Tobago went into a financial collapse. Unfortunately there was no other industry to take the place of sugar. Estates were sold for as little as ten shillings per acre and many peasants took advantage of this, leaving even less labour for the remaining estates.

The sugar crisis in the West Indies was general, but Tobago was in a particular state of depression because not enough of her soil was being cultivated and consequently capital was low. She could no longer stand alone. In January 1889 the new United Colony of Trinidad and Tobago was created and Tobago retained a subordinate legislature and separate finance. Ten years later, in January 1899, Tobago was made a Ward, that is, an administrative district of Trinidad and Tobago, losing its subordinate legislature and separate finances. A new era of history had begun.

FIRSTS IN TOBAGO

1900   First telephones installed.
1921   First motorbus plies route between Scarborough and Roxborough.
1922   Public Library established.
1923   Child Welfare League formed.
        Coastal steamer taken over by Government.
1925   Pipe-borne water supply inaugurated.
        First secondary school (Bishop's High School) opened.
        Sir William Ingram's heirs give Little Tobago to Government.
1927   Methodist Church at Charlotteville consecrated.
1930   First plane to Tobago lands at Plymouth.
1950   Barclays Bank (now Republic Bank) opened.
1952   Hillsborough waterworks opened.
1961   Sir Winston Churchill visits Tobago.
1963   Hurricane Flora hits Tobago.
1964   Queen Elizabeth and Prince Philip visit Tobago.

PART II

The people

| 3 |
True, true Tobagonian

When Christopher Columbus saw Tobago on his third voyage of discovery in 1498 and named it Assumption, it was already inhabited by Caribs and Arawaks who occupied the north-western and south-eastern portions of the island respectively. Who knows, some of them may actually have glimpsed the great navigator's ships in the distance and wondered at them, little guessing that their fate would be inextricably bound up with those passing ships in the not too distant future.

Today, 500 years later, we know how fate handled the matter and it's a little sad that except for a few anthropological relics and some place names, there remains hardly a trace of these peoples and certainly nothing of their lifestyle or features in the persons of present-day Tobagonians. In fact, by the mid-eighteenth century, when serious European settlement began, the Amerindians had almost completely died out and only about 300 of them existed.

Europe, specifically Great Britain, had a significant social and economic impact upon Tobago, but although the races did mix, producing free coloureds, the physical make-up and general complexion of the average Tobagonian is definitely African and has always been so, deriving as it does from those Africans who came as slaves.

The African population of Tobago always exceeded the number of whites by a very large amount. In 1775 for example, when the population of the island numbered about 14 000, at least 10 000 of these were Africans, and by 1807 when the trade in slaves was abolished, Tobago's African population had further increased; it was still strong when the apprenticeship system ended in 1838 and the former slaves were fully freed. It is the descendants of these freed men and women who make up the present African population of Tobago. They are a race of graceful, essentially ebony-skinned people, who have inherited many of the customs of their African ancestors.

Walking the streets of Tobago or digging the fields; planting yams on the hillsides or providing medical care for the population; working in

A house near Golden Lane *opposite* (MIKE TOY)

(PHOTO BY DONALD NAUSBAUM)

shops and stores, running their own businesses, huckstering; pulling seine on the beach, or holding public office administering the affairs of the country - one sees some of the most physically beautiful men, women and children in the world.

They are a very proud people - proud of their heritage and of their culture - and even though communications and constant contact with different cultures have greatly influenced their attitudes and lifestyle,

opposite (PHOTO BY DONALD NAUSBAUM)

there is that underlying thread – really more of an umbilical cord – which ties them to their past and generates both love and respect for their African identity. This identity has never been lost, nor does it seem to be in any danger of being lost, because Tobagonians live their African-ness. They go back to the village where their heart ties are and the land resuscitates them. They love the land that is Tobago. They rejoice in its beauty and in belonging to it. Tobago is their idea of paradise.

The island itself is rather like a large village comprised of a number of smaller villages, and the village tie is very important. There is no true, true Tobagonian who does not belong to a village, be it Windward or North Side or South East. The vital inner life of Tobago goes on in its villages – christenings, weddings, harvests, funerals – all the significant human contacts take place primarily in the village.

Two of the more important elements of Tobago's cultural configuration are kinship and love of land. Kinship ties are very strong. 'Fambly is fambly', the saying goes. Tobago is a place of 'tribes', tribes that are 'fambly'. If you belong to a tribe, you'll always belong, and other

Children at the grave of Gang Gang Sara (MIKE TOY)

tribes recognise you by the family name wherever you go. J. D. Elder, a famous Tobago historian, renowned for the work he has done among his own people, says: 'Ranking high in the value system and very crucial to community life in Tobago, is the primary family and the network of inter-familial relationships between members of kin groups.' These kin groups to which he refers are the 'tribes'.

Essentially, descent is through the male line, but a woman's family is also recognised and respected; to speak disrespectfully of one's mother or her family is thought to be very bad. However, Tobagonians consider it of fundamental benefit and importance to hear the sound of a man's voice in the home as head of the household, and women will put up with much in order to ensure that their children enjoy this benefit.

Love of land in the Tobagonian is bred into the genes. Probably as a result of their landless situation in the days of slavery, they have developed a remarkable affinity for property. From the time a child is born, parents start thinking of putting aside money for a bit of land, or for a cow, goat or sheep that will help to bring more money for the land. Having it, owning it, is the important thing. They may plant it and never build on it, but it will be there. 'Land does not spoil,' they say, and they will acquire more with time, to be handed down from one generation to the next and become ancestral land. Selling it is, more often than not, out of the question.

TOBAGO'S RADIO STATION

92.1 FM, Ah We Radio 'Tambrin' is Tobago's radio station, named after the indigenous Tobago drum which provides such a fascinating rhythm in all local affairs. It was started on 8 June 1998 and has proved to be just what Tobago has been looking for in this field, injecting the right amount of enthusiasm, generating considerable interest, and almost taking over the Tobago listeners from other radio stations in the twin island republic. It provides a forum for Tobagonians to air their views and concerns on Tobago and to obtain information and quick responses on matters that are important to them.

The service operates from 3 Picton Street, Scarborough, Tobago; e-mail: tambrin@tstt.net.tt

The rise of tourism in Tobago has put pressure on this Tobagonian principle of no sale. Demand for land is high and the offered prices good because of the dollar exchange, so the present-day conflict for the Tobagonian, who might be rich in land but 'cash poor' as the saying goes, is very real. Young people, needing money for education, business, daily living, put pressure on the older folk to sell and often win through, but their fight is never easy.

One hundred and sixteen square miles (300 sq km) of island between the Atlantic Ocean and the Caribbean Sea is not much on which to conduct world-shaking enterprise, but Tobagonians do their thing very unobtrusively, employing much thrift and know-how to make a good living for themselves. Sugar and cocoa, the original cash crops of the settler planters, have long ceased to be significant, but agriculture is practised to a considerable extent, even though the yield is not enough to satisfy the needs of the local population and must be supplemented by imports from nearby Trinidad.

Animal farming though, is very popular, and there are cows, goats, pigs and of course the ubiquitous hair sheep (you see them grazing

(PHOTO BY DONALD NAUSBAUM)

everywhere). There is no shortage of fresh meat in the market as the local government authority, the Tobago House of Assembly, familiarly called the THA, has seriously tried to develop these aspects of the economy in an attempt to help Tobago feed itself. There is hardly a yard that does not have its resident chickens, and even if not engaged in animal culture on a large scale, hardly a village homestead that does not boast sheep or goats or both. It's quite customary to see a small boy leading sheep out to pasture in the early morning, or a man or woman at evening time walking purposefully home, charges trotting along with them – without leading strings.

However, although meat is plentiful, the staple protein of your true, true Tobagonian is fish, and there's always plenty of it. Fishing is a major industry and it is the pride of the island that fresh fish is available all over the country every day. Fish is also dried, smoked and salted, a profitable cottage industry in villages like Charlotteville, where the fresh catch tends to be plentiful. At least two of the larger fish preparation factories offer dried and smoked fish for sale on a regular basis as well.

A roadside fish stall near Studley Park (MICHAEL BOURNE)

The flying fish industry (this particular fish is so named because of its habit of skimming or 'flying' over the ocean) forms a large part of Tobago's fishing enterprise and there are special factories which cut and bone the fish into fillets ready for cooking. A large amount of this flying fish is exported to Trinidad and other Caribbean islands.

Apart from these enterprises, Tobagonians do what every other people on a small island do. They work in or run small shops and stores, sell produce, work in government jobs, teach, nurse, practise medicine and law, are hoteliers and restaurateurs … you name it, they do it with pride because it's a Tobago thing. In the markets you hear: 'this is Tobago breadfruit'; 'these tomatoes grow right here!'; 'these are Tobago watermelons … pawpaws … avocados'. It is a pride which implies that the very soil of the island produces superior quality. Believe me, it does.

Fishermen pulling seine at Castara Bay *previous pages* (DONALD NAUSBAUM)

| 4 |
Food – Tobago-style

Tobagonians love food! Generations of Tobago cooks have used their traditional resources (ground provisions, meats, fish and abundant fruit), blended them imaginatively, improvised by using them with other foods and succeeded in evolving a cuisine that is lively and delightful on the palate.

There has never been a significant multicultural population in Tobago from which to draw different culinary arts, so the cooking patterns of native Tobagonians have their roots embedded deep in the African heritage of their forefathers.

Hotels and restaurants, for example Kariwak Village Hotel at Crown Point, do not concentrate on reproducing European fare. Instead, they pride themselves that they have combined the two worlds of Europe and Africa very tastefully, for their food, while delicately probing the tastebuds, also expresses the resources of a vibrant, gutsy land with rich, fertile soil bearing abundantly and seas teeming with seafood.

Tobago's traditional fare is a high-carbohydrate, deliciously spiced concoction that is as full of panache as a Moriah wedding. Special spices, herbs, and sauce-thickeners such as coconut milk and cassava flour add a devil-may-care exhilaration to this Creole cooking that sets gastric juices flowing.

Ground provisions (thus called because the part you eat grows under the ground) formed the main diet of the island's African population during slavery. There's yam, cassava, sweet potato, dasheen, tania, eddoes, cush-cush, all varying in texture and taste.

There was a time in Tobago when only well-off families could afford meat, so less fortunate housewives, left with mainly ground provisions and of course, fish, were forced to think up imaginative ways of serving these foods to their families very regularly. The more enterprising of these ladies worked with what they had, combining the ingredients with special sauces and seasonings and even with cheese, which was cheap. They made yam and cheese pies, sautéed eddoes with onions, lightly fried crushed tania seasoned with thyme and black pepper to make delicious, hot tania cakes, and used the fruit of the

dried coconut in numerous ways, thus introducing a whole new range of foods to the cooking practices of those days.

Today, these provisions are at the very top of Tobago's food list. Prepared in some special way, or simply boiled with salt to accompany meat or fish with a sauce, perhaps some rice, and a variety of beans, peas or other vegetables, they make up the average daily fare of Tobagonians. Of course, when on Sundays and special occasions, gastronomic delights such as pound plantain, macaroni pie or green banana souse are served with stewed pork and pigeon peas or chicken with coconut milk and other side dishes - well, that's food to die for!

STUFFED CHRISTOPHENE, KARIWAK VILLAGE-STYLE

3 medium-sized christophenes (chayote squash)
Two-thirds cup grated cheddar cheese
1 teaspoon minced onion
2–3 teaspoons breadcrumbs
Salt and pepper to taste
Pepper sauce – optional

- Drop the whole christophenes into boiling water and boil until cooked, or until the skin is easily pierced with a fork.
- Drain and cool.
- Cut each christophene in half lengthways and discard the seed.
- Scoop out the flesh, leaving enough around the edges to support the shell so that it can stand on its own. It takes the flesh from six halves to stuff four adequately.
- Chop the flesh by hand or using a food processor.
- Add the remaining ingredients
- Refill four shells with the mixture and sprinkle lightly with grated cheese.
- Bake at 180°C (350°F) until golden brown on top.

Vegetable stall at Scarborough market *opposite* (MIKE TOY)

The breadfruit is also a Tobagonian staple. Found in Tahiti by Captain Cook, the tree was brought to the Caribbean by Captain Bligh and now grows abundantly throughout Tobago. While the fruit of this tree is somewhat bland, it lends itself graciously to dressing up. Tobagonians are very fond of breadfruit and think themselves fortunate to own a tree, because, they say, their children will never starve with a breadfruit tree in the yard.

A good meal is easy to come by on the island. Apart from the hotels and restaurants which cover the evening trade particularly, there are other hotels, for example Kariwak Village, which serve a great lunch. There are also smaller food places, especially in Scarborough and Store Bay, where during the day local women do a good trade selling meals in easy-to-spot wayside shops; you can either eat on the premises or take away. Two of the most popular venues are located in the Scarborough market and at the Store Bay facility near the beach. Local cooks at both venues compete for patronage, serving absolutely, undilutedly, grassroots food such as curried crab and dumplins,

Roadside stalls (MICHAEL BOURNE)

steamed or fried fish with callaloo and coo-coo (made of ground corn and ochroes), and a number of other titbits such as cassava pone and coconut drops.

These stalls are patronised by locals and visitors alike, and those at the market have a breakfast trade as well of smoked herring, fried fish and salt fish buljol (dried fish with olive oil, onions and tomatoes), with avocado on the side when in season, served with home-made bread, fried bake or roast coconut bake. There's tea, coffee and of course, local Tobago cocoa, which has been grated and boiled with spices, a speciality in itself. Miss Virgie at her stall in the centre of the market provides ready-made cocoa balls complete with a cocoa-making recipe, to warm the cockles of hearts in wintertime.

As elsewhere in the Caribbean, Tobagonians love the pungent, burning tang of pepper. The Amerindians were making a hot mixture with peppers long before Columbus's sailing adventure, and the taste for that fiery stuff has hung around in Tobago, where we concoct different versions of pepper sauce using sour cherries, coreilli, carrot or christophene, cauliflower and even salad beans in a ground or sliced pepper base, with vinegar and sometimes mustard. Many of these sauces are very hot, but there are market vendors who make them with flavour peppers, a not-hot variety of pepper that has a good flavour. Most people take pepper sauce with their food almost automatically, and it's especially important in fish broth and other seafood dishes.

Being an island positively guarantees an abundance of seafood. On most beaches from Charlotteville to Scarborough, on both shores, one can buy the fish that's biting (taking the bait at that time), be it snapper, kingfish, shark, bonito, carite or barracuda, not to mention dolphin (the fish, not the mammal), grouper and the wonderful flying fish! It's a delight to pull up at a beach and watch the men as they pull in a seine, or bring in the day's catch from their boats. Both the dolphin and king-fish have turned a dark pewter grey by the time they reach consumers, but sometimes if you catch the boats as they come in, you get to see before they fade the glorious turquoise blue, silver, vermilion and gold hues that these creatures flaunt in their natural habitat.

Conch, a sea creature that lives in a hard shell, is another popular food. It's rather rubbery, but when curried or stewed (with coconut, naturally) or used in a salad, it's very good. It's as good as the crabs, which are served in various ways but mainly as curried crab and dumplin, or in callaloo. Sometimes too they're simply steamed and enjoyed. The callaloo is a thick, green soup made from the leaf of the

Red snapper fresh from the sea (MICHAEL BOURNE)

dasheen plant cooked with okra and seasonings such as thyme, chives, onions and garlic, with a bit of pumpkin and coconut milk, and of course a large, hot, red pepper that only the brave at heart will allow to burst while the soup is simmering. Normal mortals prefer to keep the pepper whole and save the roofs of their mouths from shouting!

In imitation of the salted cod or haddock which is used to make buljol, there is a local variety of salted and smoked fish prepared in the same way by certain households in the island, particularly in Charlotteville. Many families make a good living from this cottage industry. Preserved in this way, the fish lasts a very long time and can be cooked exactly as codfish, adding yet more evidence of the ability and imagination of Tobagonians in making the best use of their food resources.

Different types of food play different roles in the life of Tobago. 'Pacroe water' is the island's 'totally local' food. There's really no other name for it, because it's the broth in which a small brown sea urchin, known as 'pacroe' or sea cockroach, has been boiled. The water is supposed to have restorative aphrodisiac qualities for both males and females and is sold in Scarborough by male vendors particularly, who carry it around in large buckets shouting, 'Pacroe!'

Yet another seafood aphrodisiac is whelks. The creature here lives in an attractive silver and black shell, and it's sold as it is, shell and all. This delicacy is not so easy to get, unless you can recognise the brown crocus bag in which they're being transported, and there's a science to proper cleaning and preparation, but whelks are truly delicious when prepared by someone who knows how. Then there's 'goat water', sometimes called 'mannish water', which is another aphrodisiac favourite, prepared by cooking special parts of a male goat. The name says it all, I guess.

A spin-off from the local butchering of animals is the black pudding and souse trade. These are essentially weekend delicacies, because most of the butchering is done on a Thursday, in preparation for weekend market. They're usually available at special street corners, near bars and supermarkets. A well-known, well-tried vendor sells her wares in front

The Old Donkey Cart House Restaurant, Bacolet (MIKE TOY)

49

LEMON CAULIFLOWER WITH FRESH DILL

4 servings

1 lb (500 g) clean cauliflower florets
3 tablespoons butter
2 teaspoons onion, minced
1 small clove garlic, crushed
Three-quarters teaspoon curry powder
1 tablespoon lemon juice
2 tablespoons fresh dill
Salt and pepper to taste

- Sauté onion, curry and garlic in 1 tablespoon butter.
- Cool and stir in the remaining 2 tablespoons butter.
- Add lemon juice, salt and pepper.
- Steam cauliflower until tender but crisp.
- Toss warm cauliflower with butter mixture.
- Toss in dill and serve.

of Pennysaver's Supermarket in Canaan - not before four o'clock, though. Black pudding is blood pudding, and souse is a pickled form of either pig's trotters and face, chicken feet, or cow's face. The demand by locals is very high, this being an important aspect of either Saturday night's dinner or Sunday morning's breakfast, or both!

Green vegetables add that other important dimension to the local cuisine. Most of them are not grown locally, but in the sister isle, Trinidad. However, local farmers do manage to produce some - just not enough to go around. The usual vegetables are cauliflower, christophene, carrots, cabbage, sweet peppers, corn, tomatoes and beans. These are used in salads or as side dishes, and as usual the Creole touch enlivens them considerably. Many hotels and restaurants invent exciting ways with vegetables, as shown in the two recipes from the Kariwak Village Hotel above and on page 45.

Many delicious desserts satisfy Tobago's 'sweet tooth'. For the average Tobagonian, home-made ice-cream is usually the favourite; coconut flavour, preferably. It's usually served with fruit cake or sponge cake, and sometimes bread pudding, or even pone, which itself is a type of baked pudding made with grated cassava, sweet potato, coconut,

La Tartaruga Restaurant, Buccoo village (MIKE TOY)

pumpkin, and lots of sugar, spices and raisins. There are also coconut drops, a thick biscuit with plenty of grated coconut; sugar cakes with a touch of ginger; green papaya balls and tamarind balls; and starch cakes, an old Tobago recipe actually made from the starch extracted from grated cassava.

Tall cool drinks with ice run to lemonade and lime squash; sour-sop punch; mauby (made from a bitter bark); sea-moss, using a special type of sea-weed; sorrel drink from the flowers of a hibiscus relative, the sorrel plant; ginger beer; and lots of home-made fruit wines. Ginger beer and sorrel are made primarily at Christmas, for the tart flavour of the red sorrel drink and slight heat of the ginger beer go well with the salty Christmas ham. Fresh fruit juices come from a variety of citrus and other fruits such as watermelon, papaya, pineapple, and so on, and in numerous island bars you can have them tinged with just the right amount of alcohol to make very exotic drinks.

| 5 |
Politics and government

The islands of Trinidad and Tobago are connected politically, in that they are one nation, under one flag. In colonial times Tobago was governed by England and was, in the late nineteenth century, attached to Trinidad. That attachment was not desired by either island but was thrust upon them by British authority to suit its own convenience. At the time when the attachment took place, Tobago's ties to Trinidad were not at all extensive. She had closer connections with Barbados and Grenada than with Trinidad, but because Trinidad was geographically closer the two were brought together, much to the general displeasure of Tobago's population – a displeasure which still manifests itself today.

An 1816 Tobago Coat of Arms.
The legend reads: 'She becomes more beautiful'

The Seal of Tobago

The two islands are not alike in the least. There is nothing of one that brings the other to mind. They happen to be geographically close to each other, but share neither a common historical experience nor a joint heritage and their populations are very different. The way of life, culture, ideology - all of these are different.

After its attachment in 1889 Tobago was at first governed completely from Trinidad, but it was a constant battle, for many of the island's interests were left untended and there was an unfair disparity in the benefits given to its citizens and those given to the citizens of Trinidad; there were many Tobagonians who even then were demanding self-government. From the earliest days a series of attempts at providing some form of resident administration in Tobago were made. These progressed from the stage of the Warden, whose role was more or less that of a Governor, to having a Commissioner for Tobago Affairs and a Ministry for Tobago Affairs, but none of these solutions worked. The problems remained the same and others accrued.

By 1980 the people of Tobago, or perhaps one should say the people of Trinidad and Tobago, had to come to terms with a new political reality regarding Tobago. The Tobago House of Assembly Act No 37 of 1980 established the House of Assembly as a unique entity, with the stated objective of making better provision for the overall administration of the island than had been made before. In other words, the Assembly had been created to provide for the needs, aspirations and general well-being of the people of Tobago, in all aspects of their lives. Self-determination was a reality

Back in 1976, the Member in the Parliament of Trinidad and Tobago for Tobago East, the Honourable A. N. R. Robinson, himself a well-loved son of Tobago soil, had tabled a motion asking that internal self-government be granted to the island which was, at that time, part of the Unitary State of Trinidad and Tobago.

Mr Robinson's motion had been timed to coincide with the national general election of 1976 and in that election, the electorate of Tobago totally rejected the People's National Movement, the ruling

A. N. R. Robinson (left), with former US President Jimmy Carter (POPPERFOTO)

political party running the nation's government at the time. As a result of this rejection the angry central government dismantled the Ministry of Tobago Affairs, which had since 1960 been administering the island's affairs. Confusion resulted and Tobago experienced considerable difficulties. Her demand for self-determination was a response to the situation. The island had never wanted to be attached to Trinidad in the first place and had always felt that she had lost economically in the exchange of benefits. She wanted to manage her own affairs.

Monument outside the Tobago House of Assembly (DONALD NAUSBAUM)

The request for internal self-government was aimed at removing the hardships and inequalities suffered by the people of Tobago by providing for them to administer their own affairs as they saw fit.

In 1990, on the occasion of the tenth anniversary of the formation of the Tobago House of Assembly, the Prime Minister of the Nation of Trinidad and Tobago, A. N. R. Robinson, wrote: 'The inauguration of the Tobago House of Assembly on 4 December 1980 was an event of singular importance in the history of Trinidad and Tobago. Not only did it recognise the distinctiveness of Tobago's history, of which Tobagonians are justly proud, but it also symbolised the recognition of the fundamental right of peoples to self-determination.'

He further said that the House of Assembly, which had taken its character and strength and personality from the people of Tobago, was an organic infusion of the aspirations of those same people, and that the very existence of the THA encompassed centuries of history and culture, welded into an institution which represented the hopes of its people.

When the Act of 1980 came into force, it became the responsibility of the Tobago House of Assembly to assist the central government in its formation and implementation of policies in specific areas of administration and development in Tobago, including the compilation of estimates that were to be submitted to the central government. However, in 1996 this Act was repealed and replaced by a new Tobago House of Assembly Act which was to provide for the membership, powers and functions of the THA, its new Executive Council and all matters related thereto.

There are now 12 elected Assemblymen and four Councillors and there is provision also for a Presiding Officer who may or may not be an Assemblyman or Councillor. These Assemblymen have been elected by the people of Tobago in a local election process contested by national political parties and it is the electorate that decides which party will obtain majority seats and thus govern the House of Assembly, and which will be in the minority and consequently form the opposition.

After the election the Assemblymen have the responsibility to elect from among themselves the Chief Secretary and the Deputy Chief Secretary of the gathering. Following these two appointments, a Minority Leader is appointed. This is the Assemblyman who in the opinion of the President commands the support of the largest number of Assemblymen who do not support the Chief Secretary; the Minority Leader can thus lead the opposition in the House.

After the swearing-in of the Minority Leader by the President of t. Republic, the Presiding Officer, under advice from the Chief Secretary, appoints three Councillors and then one more under the advice of the Minority Leader, thus making four Councillors in all.

Under the new Act, the functions and powers of the Assembly have increased and broadened and the body has been given full rein in the exercise of its powers to do what is necessary for the effective running of the island. It is able to devise means to protect its property, buildings or assets; enter into contracts as it deems fit for efficient discharge of its function; obtain aid, grants or technical assistance from international donors; and propose and adopt Bills in relation to matters for which it is responsible. These Bills are known as Assembly Bills.

It is also responsible for the provision, maintenance and control of public areas such as burial grounds, markets and recreation grounds. It gives assistance to community, district and village councils and provides and maintains roads, buildings, health and sanitation in the island, as well as being responsible for promoting sport, culture and marketing of commodities. Individual secretaries (there are seven of them appointed by the Chief Secretary) are responsible for the administration of specific areas and they, with the Deputy Chief Secretary, are responsible to the Chief Secretary.

Flag of Trinidad and Tobago

enses incurred by the Assembly, including the salaries of its
re paid from a fund - the Tobago House of Assembly fund -
s established under the earlier Act of 1980 for that very pur-
e monies are provided by the Parliament of the Republic out
appointed for the servicing of the financial year, and are
directly related to estimates submitted to the Cabinet of Trinidad and
Tobago by the island's Chief Secretary.

Regardless of its powers in relation to the administration of Tobago,
however, the Tobago House of Assembly has no authority in regard
to matters pertaining to the Republic of Trinidad and Tobago and
furthermore, still rests under the control of the National Parliament.
Considering that no control whatsoever from Trinidad is desired by
Tobago, this state of affairs seriously exacerbates the tension between
the two islands.

Under the 1980 Act it is important, if not vital, that the two entities,
central government and the Tobago House of Assembly, co-operate and
consult with each other and assist each other as the need arises.

Coat of Arms of Trinidad and Tobago

However, the problem is that neither side can claim that the new relationship runs smoothly, and the new powers granted in the Act which seemed so extensive have been referred to as 'illusory'. There have even been calls from those in both camps who despair of the situation for a complete severance, which would give Tobago its independence. Money and ideology rest at the heart of the matter.

The political realities of each island do not help the situation at all. It is absolutely possible, because of the fact that two separate islands are involved, that the Tobago House of Assembly could be run by a group that belongs to a political party that is totally opposed to the party which forms the Government of Trinidad and Tobago, that is, the central government. It is not the Government of Trinidad and Tobago that elects the THA, but the people of Tobago. The people of Trinidad have no say in the matter, although Tobago has a say in the results of the general elections of the nation, in that there are two Tobago seats to be disputed - Tobago East and Tobago West. In the 1995 general election it was those Tobago seats, obtained by one party, the United National Congress, then in its deadlock situation with the People's National Movement, that allowed the UNC to emerge victorious as the Government of Trinidad and Tobago.

So the situation is very complex, and the natural disagreements of political parties only tend to confuse the issue further, because each party has its own agenda. Will the problem ever be solved? Political pundits on both islands ponder this.

| 6 |
Festivals and celebrations

Carnival

Carnival is the earliest festival in the Trinidad and Tobago calendar year. It takes place before the start of the Lenten season. Want to see Tobago Carnival? Be there for the Monday and Tuesday before Ash Wednesday, in any year of your choice. Those are the Carnival days. The Carnival season, however, is another matter. That starts at the beginning of January. Calypso tents on both islands open and the bards of calypso, known as calypsonians, entertain the nation with their songs, vying for public appreciation which at its zenith will lead one of them to being crowned King of Calypso for the current year. Such is the ambition of every calypsonian in this twin island state.

The season's programme is jam-packed with events, which are all driven by the music of that year as produced by the calypsonians. These men and women are the very heart of Carnival, for from them come the songs and music to which the country sizzles for the entire season. They bring out the laughter and joy, the energy and exhilaration, that are the essence of Carnival.

There are steelband competitions and concerts, there are numerous fêtes - public and private, there's brass band music and disc jockeys who play all the latest calypso music available on tape or CD for their audiences. It's a go, go, go season! One can go with the flow, or one can define a personal pace: participate, look on, or simply ignore it all. That's the Carnival season.

Carnival itself is an extremely old festival dating back to pre-Emancipation days, when exclusively the upper-class white and free coloured population enjoyed it. It was only after Emancipation that the black population became a part of Carnival.

The start of Carnival on Monday morning is J'Ouvert. 'Jour ouvert' is pronounced 'jouvay', meaning daybreak. According to the literature on the subject, the origin of the term derives from a folk tale about a *soucouyant* or blood sucker - always referred to as being female - who sheds her human skin at midnight to roam the land in search of

Tobago Carnival: old mas' *opposite* (STEVE COHEN TRAVEL)

victims on whose blood she must survive. But she knows that her time for this pleasure is limited. Daybreak - jour ouvert - must not catch her *sans* skin. She must resume her natural form. However, the soucouyant of the tale is unable to put her skin back on because someone has sprinkled salt on it, and everyone knows, *salt is anathema to a soucouyant!* As day approaches our soucouyant is left crying 'jouvay, jou paka ouvre?' which is the patois for 'daybreak, or no daybreak?'

Sometime after 1884, when folklore characters began appearing on the streets at Carnival time in the dark of early morning, acting out their parts as nocturnal creatures who could not stand the light of day, the term jouvay came to be identified with Carnival and was used to describe these types of masks. As time passed, fewer of these folklore characters appeared and jouvay was taken over by old mask characters. Old mas' became the traditional mask played at this part of the Carnival and has remained thus.

Old mas', as its name implies, is not a fancy mask with beautiful costumes, but a seemingly put-together affair, where maskers not only use deliberately odd-looking garments made of rags, paper, flour bags, old cans, old plastic bottles and more (you name it, they use it), but also bits and pieces of their Carnival costumes from previous years. The aim is to be humorous or decrepit-looking. No one and nothing escapes the incisive old mas' satire and humour. It comments on whatever occurs in the country, crime, politics, love … It is no respecter of persons and its wit lies not only in the idea being portrayed - 'have you ever seen a *side* walk?' - but in the mimed performances and the absurd garments of those doing the portrayal.

Such is the traditional old mas' session of Carnival Trinidad and Tobago, but Tobago, where generally the Carnival is not as hectic as in Trinidad, has emphasised a particularly exciting variety of old mas' which is called mud mas', where soil and water mixed together to the consistency of mud is actually a costume!

The emphasis on this type of mask for most of Carnival Monday gives a special quality to the Tobago celebrations. Old mas' is generally less organised and more informal than fancy mas', but mud mas' makes for even greater freedom, if that's possible.

The mud is specially prepared. Mud mas' practitioners get together in backyards to mix the mud they will use. Soil that has been collected from different parts of the island is put into separate, large oil drums with boiling water. Separation matters because soil from different places varies in colour and quality. Moriah, for example has a dark soil while Calder Hall's is cream and Patience Hill's is red. Even though coated in mud, maskers have an identity! Once mixed, the mud is stirred frequently until Carnival to prevent settling, and to it is added some form of purifier as protection for the maskers' skins.

Carnival Monday morning in Tobago. Daybreak. Cocks crowing, cocricos squawking in the bushes, the steelbands coming out. Maskers – mud mas', old mas', devils, jab-jabs – join in. The tintinnabulation of the pans rises above the revellers like morning mist over the Main Ridge. The Atlantic roars its acquiescence. Down the roads they go, converging on downtown Scarborough. The revelry has started. Tobago is under siege by yet another monarch. King Carnival reigns!

Tuesday is the day of whatever fancy costumed bands there are, bands being groups of people who get together to portray the same theme, moving to the steelband or some other form of music. The children's carnival and its competition are important parts of this day. There are many children's bands and it's truly delightful to see these blossoming exponents of the art of mas' playing, dressed in their gay costumes, waving flags, banners, spears as they chip to the rhythms, having the time of their lives. Of course, make no mistake: the adults are doing the same thing – playing mas' – for that's what the Carnival is all about!

Easter celebrations

Easter is school vacation time, when Trinidadians flock to Tobago to soak in the sun and participate in festivities. The Easter Monday goat race and sports at Mount Pleasant and the Easter Tuesday goat and crab races at Buccoo draw the crowd like magnets. This is fun with a very big difference! Dogs are motivated to run with a bone, but what does one use to motivate a goat to go charging along? A whip? Perhaps, but although the 'jockeys' carry switches, they hardly ever use them. These Tobago goats have been so well trained to race that they're eager to do it. Once the gates fly, they're off!

Both Mount Pleasant and Buccoo are popular venues, but Buccoo, being the first place to entertain the event in 1925, has the edge in the popularity stakes. It was a Barbadian, Mr Samuel Callendar, who introduced the goat race to Buccoo 75 years ago. Buccoo is just a small village with a population of approximately 1500 people, but she has become quite famous as a result of her offshore reef and Nylon Pool, which attract thousands of visitors each year from all over the world.

Goat racing (TRIP/M. JELIFFE)

Easter Tuesday is an unofficial half-holiday in Tobago: while the rest of the country goes back to work, Tobago goes to the goat races. According to an official race card:

In Tobago, Good Friday and Easter Saturday were chosen for marble pitching. Easter Sunday was the Moravian Love Feast. Easter Monday was for horse racing at Petit Trou Beach. Prizes for the 1925 Goat Race were marbles, which created a source of excitement, with the outstanding goat owners and runners sharing the prizes.

That left Easter Tuesday for goat racing - naturally.

Horse racing is no longer held in Tobago, but goat and crab racing continue unabated and other race days have been added. At both venues the occasion has the atmosphere of a village fair. The racing takes place on the only available flat, clear ground and the crowd, young and old, come intent upon enjoyment.

64

The goats are groomed to perfection. There are no raggedy-looking creatures here! These are the aristocrats of the genre. Their coats are shining and smooth, brushed to glistening perfection. Horns have been polished and decorated with gay ribbons. A jockey, or more precisely a runner, runs alongside each animal, guiding it with a rope and coaxing it with a slim switch, and the race is as much a test of his endurance as it is of the goat's. Once the gates fly they're off, amidst the cheering and shouting of the crowd, which, by the way, has been betting quite briskly on the outcome. There are at least eight or ten races and all the appurtenances of horse racing, including an announcer.

Crab racing, although understandably far less physical for the 'jockey', is just as exciting. Crabs, it seems, never develop a feel for the sport like goats do, possibly because one, they have no residual memory of having done it before and two, in the normal way of things they scurry rather than run.

The crab race, then, is run sideways because that's how crabs walk! The jockey guides the crab by a string tied to its body and contrives to prevent the creature from bolting down the nearest hole, or for that matter, getting hold of someone's toe with its claws! He also uses a light stick to guide the creature in the direction of the winning post, but this is not easy, as apart from being strictly sideways scramblers, crabs are also quite single-minded and intent upon escape. The first crab to cross the line, facing whichever way, wins. The race ends amidst general laughter and conviviality. Bets are collected and the crabs ... well, we do know that unlike the goats, they don't go home until next time. There's a saying in the islands: 'If crab nah walk, he no get fat' - for the pot, that is!

Harvest festivals

Village harvest festivals are cosy, authentic expressions of the Tobago way of life. They take place on Sundays very frequently during the year. I remember someone saying to me that there's a harvest celebration in Tobago every Sunday. Well, it's not really as frequent as that, but they do turn up pretty regularly.

The harvest is strictly a village affair. Each village has one harvest day - always a Sunday - which is constant every year, and for the villagers it involves cooking enormous amounts of food. Usually the men do the cooking. Women are the hostesses, serving guests and making them comfortable. They welcome friends, family, visitors and even passing strangers into their homes, offering food and drink and hospitality. This is one of the very few occasions when one gets to see Tobagonians at home. It's all home style. What the home has, it offers, willingly. And it's very charming and heartwarming, particularly to those whose homes are in distant lands.

The food is traditional Tobago diet, unsophisticated but delicious. It can be cow head or pork cooked in a variety of ways, wild meat such as iguana or manicou, beef, chicken cou-cou, ground provisions, green fig, plantain, etc.

Harvests are church-based. In most villages there's a special church service with a cantata and the rest of the day is spent in preparing for one's visitors, although many efficient households have the preparation well in advance ahead of time.

In very long-ago days harvests were essentially a feature of church life, the Methodist and Anglican Church, that is. One brought to the church house as an offering on the Saturday the best of one's produce from the land. On harvest day, Sunday, the churches would be laden with bananas, coconuts, cocoa, yams and other produce that would be sold in the schoolroom on Monday, and the money would go into the church's coffers. It was the people's way of saying thank you to God. Later on when visiting started, it was men, not women, who did the visiting. They would arrive in the village, dressed for church service in black suits. The women of the village wore newly made beautiful white dresses, which they changed, after service, for coloured dresses, and went out deliberately, not exactly to parade, but definitely to give the neighbours an eyeful. Children could expect to have new outfits 'from top to toe' as they say, meaning hats and shoes included.

Some think that the visiting and entertainment features of the harvests started in the east of Tobago, possibly in Pembroke. There were large cocoa plantations and estates in the east and money for entertaining guests was more available, particularly when the cess (payment for the cocoa by the Government) was paid to the planters. Gradually, though, the practice moved westwards.

Much of the past harvest activity has changed. Churches no longer collect produce for sale, and some villages have dropped the afternoon cantata, people being unwilling to come out to church again at three o'clock. But the morning church service remains and the bonhomie and gentle simplicity of the harvest persists in the genuineness of the hospitality and welcome afforded visitors, and after all, it is still an expression of thanksgiving for abundance. How does one find out which village is holding harvest on any given Sunday? Just ask people will know.

Heritage Festival

Heritage Festival outstrips all other Tobago festivals in popularity. It is infinitely more important to Tobagonians than Carnival and it allows for greater mixing and mingling among the people than Christmas, which is essentially a family affair. Every year, since its inauguration in 1987, it re-enacts various aspects of Tobago's folk heritage, the age-old traditions and practices – particularly African – in which most Tobagonians have been nurtured.

Such is the nature of Heritage that it serves to nourish the Tobagonian psyche. It reminds people of their roots and presents life in those far-gone days of slavery and post-slavery in ways which appeal to present-day Tobagonians, making them relive and further appreciate the tales of survival and experience told by their parents and grand-parents.

The Festival spans a period of 14 days at the end of July and the beginning of August each year. Participating villages usually enact their contributions on their home ground, that is, within the village itself, at a time allocated to them by the Heritage Committee. This affords visitors the pleasure of being able to absorb local colour directly within the village and also to participate in the fun and excitement that is bursting through every crevice of the place. Village cooks, proud of their 'sweet han', get an opportunity to show off their culinary *savoir faire* with dishes for which the area may be well recognised, and they take good advantage of this.

Hundreds attend these shows. I have stood in pouring rain at night at Table Piece (curious name that, but you'll understand when you see it), sharing an umbrella with an old man, to watch Les Coteaux village put on its extremely popular 'Folk Tales and Superstitions', refusing, with the rest of the crowd, to allow the weather to spoil the fun! I have also been in the small, tightly packed 'church' in Moriah for the annual dramatisation of the now famous Moriah Wedding, and believe me it is drama indeed! A Saturday morning wedding, this mock occasion is, with bride and groom in full wedding regalia exchanging solemn vows, witnessed by their 'wedding guests' – women dressed to the nines in long gowns of lace, silk or taffeta and broad-rimmed hats with streamers, not to mention fancy shoes and gloves, and men

Heritage festival dancers (STEVE COHEN TRAVEL)

elegantly set out in black scissor-tailed coats with top hats and tall black umbrellas.

After the ceremony we have all taken the wedding procession on the road and to the tune of tambrin and fiddle, danced the 'brush back' down to the wedding reception grounds – a delightful experience. The bride's godfather makes a speech which has the audience roaring with laughter at the words he uses – long, 'confabulatory' words that no dictionary knows, but which express his meaning as clearly as if Webster had recorded them.

As at all Heritage gatherings, the range of food is superb. All the old Tobago favourites appear: provisions and pound plantain, concotay (a cassava coo-coo), breadfruit balls, pork, fish, beef, chicken – a culinary history, which is also a part of the island's heritage.

Les Coteaux and Moriah are high on the Heritage favourites list but

Folk dancers at Bonkers, Toucan Inn, Crown Point (MIKE TOY)

there are, in any given year, about 17 villages taking part and Tobagonians are willing and eager to enjoy what each has to offer. Village rivalry is high, but so too is the level of fun.

The fiddle, the tambrin and the drum are the major instruments of Heritage music, and the drum especially is very evident at the Salaka Feast in Pembroke, a re-enactment of a traditional African feast, with much drumming and dancing to honour ancestors. An essential part of this event is the ceremonial roasting of a pig, which is done earlier in the day. The meat is available for sale by show time.

Plymouth is famous for its Old Time Carnival with speech bands and moko jumbie, and Roxborough, Tobago's second largest town, has its Belmanna Riots. All in all, Heritage Festival comes off as a wonderfully satisfying time for participants and viewers alike, giving visitors the opportunity of experiencing some of the things which are so uniquely Tobagonian about Tobago.

Great Race and Carnival Fest

After Heritage, Tobago moves straight to Great Race time, an annual powerboats affair, and then on to September and a new festival, a Carnival Fest which, for the past three years, has been picking up pace. This is run by the National Carnival Band Leaders Association of Tobago, and is an attempt to bring visitors to the island out of season, to ease the strain of the lean months which all tourist destinations endure. This event may make Tobago into the only place in the world with three carnival parades.

The festival lasts for three days, Friday, Saturday and Sunday. There's a Tobago Fest Queen's show on Friday night; Saturday is the day of the costumed bands street parade of adults' and children's bands, produced through the joint efforts of Trinidadian and Tobagonian band leaders; and Sunday sees the big party at Store Bay with beer-drinking competitions and the like.

Christmas

The next important time for Tobagonians on their annual calendar is, of course, Christmas. Like everywhere else in the world where it's celebrated, it's essentially a family time. The shopping for gifts and food, decorations, the excitement of children, the expectations, church worship, these are all part of Tobago's Christmas. Expressed differently, yes, but adding up to the same thing: togetherness at Christmas time.

'Christmas today is not like Christmas of yesteryear,' the old folks mourn, but they admit that churches are still packed on Christmas Eve and Christmas morning: it's still a time of sharing and joy with family and friends. Not as many kites take to the sky in the Christmas breeze as used to in the old days, but there's still laughter and merriment and Christmas smells of black cake, boiled ham and roast pork.

It's a beautiful time of year. There are blue skies and a healthy sun with scattered showers, terrific sunsets and the ever-beckoning turquoise to deep blue seas.

| 7 |
Sporting grounds

West Indians are a very sporting people. There is a saying in these islands:'Mango don't fall far from the tree.' In other words, we are much alike in many ways. Tobago is very different in many respects from other islands, but when it comes to sport, its attachment is like everyone else's. Its sport mangoes don't fall far from the Caribbean tree either, for Tobagonians are keenly interested in games of all types, as spectators and as participants. Without doubt, football and cricket are their favourite games.

Boys playing football (DONALD NAUSBAUM)

Football

Even on a small island there are numerous places to play football, some of them quite original. There are wide, flat beaches (at high or low tide) and narrow beaches at low tide only, for example Store Bay at Crown Point; there are muddy savannah grounds in the middle of a heavy downpour of rain (this is a top favourite) and the centre of a country lane or village street, using mini goal posts (mini being three and a half feet by two feet (1 by 0.7 m)) of wood and netting – or players' trainers or boots, one pair at each end of the 'field', to define the goal areas. Rainy season or dry season, there's always a football contest going on somewhere on the island.

There is of course a true football season – the rainy season, June to December – but football or its close relative, 'kicking ball', is a game that young men in Tobago feel like playing most of the time. 'Kicking ball' is just like football but there's no referee and no penalty for 'being outside'. Women usually take strong objection to it being played on a beach because it gets in the way of sunbathing, but men are quite likely to join in the game.

The island's most famous sportsman is Manchester United's multi-million dollar player Dwight Yorke and it is generally accepted in Tobago's world that the island's conditions have made and bred the sportsman that he is: that local food engendered the stamina and strength behind that powerful kick; that Tobago soil still clings to him in some magical way, goading him to greatness; that special Tobago mother's love which is like no other has blessed him; and that kinship and bonhomie – 'ah we Boy' – has enlivened his performances. In other words, his talent for the game is totally attributed to Tobago the island. This is most probably right! How else could a simple village boy become an international football star worth so many millions?

Heroes inspire, and there is no young man in Tobago kicking a ball and watching it sail through the air who does not carry in his heart the dream of being another Dwight Yorke.

Apart from the unorthodox locations for play given earlier, there are also standard football grounds and stands in which organised clubs and teams play formal games. Every village field also has its football games on a regular basis. Primary and secondary schools compete in various classes. Clubs compete with each other and with the arch-rival of all lying just 21 miles (34 km) across the Atlantic – Trinidad. Sister isle she

Dwight Yorke *opposite* (EMPICS)

is, yes, but she is also the prime object of competition. Inter-village competitions are exciting, draw large crowds and promote healthy inter-village camaraderie, because, remember, it's a small place and there's no village unto itself alone – there are always people in it who originated in other villages. But a game with a Trinidad team? Well! 'We shall have no mercy,' Tobago says, 'give no quarter.' It certainly livens things up.

There was a time when Tobago's Signal Hill team repeatedly won the national, that is, the Trinidad and Tobago Secondary School competition, but once out of school, their players did not continue to play seriously. Even so, football statistics say that there are more than 25 sons of Tobago's soil playing in the semi-professional league in Trinidad. However, the development of the sport in Tobago itself consistently suffers from lack of competition at a good level. The cost of trainers, and of travel to Trinidad or to Tobago for teams from either island, are major factors to consider.

But the situation is improving. English teams have started coming to Tobago in their off-season to practise and to survey the local talent, so local players are beginning to get the experience and the competition they need, right in their own backyard. The difficulty for the home ground is that once players develop they must migrate if they wish to grow further. Some, having been discovered by visiting teams, now play in Trinidad; others pursue professional careers in Venezuela and wherever else needs them. The ability is there, but the opportunities are wanting. There are not enough of these to go around.

Cricket

Cricket is the most popular sport in the whole chain of Caribbean islands. Horse racing may be the sport of kings, but cricket is the sport of West Indians. (It is rumoured that we grow cricketers here in some shady Caribbean grove, where our young men go to learn the art of spin and toss and sending a ball to the boundary, not to mention taking your wicket ...)

White cricket gear has that singular advantage of looking great against the undulating green of playing fields, and in every Tobago village there is a well-worn turf for inter-village and inter-club games where white-clad young men show off their batting and bowling form.

The Tobago Cricket Association sees to basics and the development of the game by promoting international games on the island and host-

Cricket on the beach (CORBIS)

ing regional teams – visiting English clubs and adult and youth teams from Trinidad. It also supports Tobago cricketers at coaching schools in England, all with the aim of upgrading the skills and techniques of the Tobago cricketers by exposing them to direct coaching by experts and to the art of the game as practised by some of its best exponents.

The results have been reasonable, but as with football, Tobago keenly feels the lack of good competitive cricket, especially at school level. The cost of getting teams to and from Tobago on a regular basis to take part in national competitions in Trinidad demands sponsorship, which can sometimes be an uphill climb. The cost of equipment, limited professional playing facilities, and a scarcity of personnel to train young people are all factors in the cricket scenario, but Tobago is not unrepresented on national teams. Players have indeed been selected to participate in inter-regional games, and the House of Assembly's efforts to link the game to tourism have brought even more visiting teams and sparked the interest of local players, giving latent talent and ability an opportunity for display.

Cricket has not yet gained the popularity which football enjoys, but the cricketing genes must still be present. Cyril Merry, who played for the West Indies in the first test at Lords and the third test at Kensington Oval, Barbados, in 1933, was the first Tobagonian to play test cricket, and Lincoln Roberts played test cricket in Jamaica in 1999. A great deal of time passed between those two games, it's true, but despite the difficulties attending the game in Tobago, the promise of improvement and development is there.

Other sports

Organised sport began in Tobago in 1980, when the responsibility for the provision and maintenance of recreational and sport facilities in the several districts of Tobago devolved upon the Tobago House of Assembly. It had previously been the responsibility of the Tobago County Council. The switch resulted eventually in the establishment of the Tobago Sports Council, whose aims are to encourage and promote all aspects of sport at all levels in the island.

Sport development is being seen now as a village-centred activity that aims at unearthing 'gifted' individuals. As a result there are six sports districts each of which enjoys full membership in the Council, whose powers are delegated equally between them. These groups have forged ahead, promoting special awards, athletics (field and track) clinics, lawn tennis clinics for children and adults, as well as a revival of track and field competitions and an inter-village draughts competition. (Travelling through Tobago, one regularly sees men playing draughts, sometimes in a village yard or under an almond tree by the sea; it is a special Tobago pastime.)

Over the years, lawn tennis programmes including coaching clinics and tournaments for adults and schools have been promoted with the aid of business corporations and while there are not many playing acilities, there is a public court in Scarborough which visitors may use as well and where they may even enjoy a night game; most of the big hotels have tennis courts.

Netball has always been a favourite Tobagonian women's sport, and has responded to the new benefits of seminars and financial assistance that have come its way. Skills have improved and there is now an even

Mount Irvine Golf Course, one of the Caribbean's finest *opposite* (MIKE TOY)

greater public interest and awareness of the sport, accompanied by stronger rivalry between the teams.

Golf brings us to the sport whose participants are essentially non-local. Not that there aren't local exponents of the art; there are, but not many. The beautiful Mount Irvine Golf Course attached to the Mount Irvine Hotel – across the street from one of the most delightful stretches of turquoise-blue sea in the world – is a famous 18-hole championship course which attracts players from far and wide, and there are other courses being planned as well.

Cycling is very popular and Tobago does have a cycling champion of its own, a national champion at that. For those who just like biking as a personal sport there are always rented bikes and motorbikes, but be careful: the roads are narrow and there are many cars.

Shaw Park, an open arena in Scarborough that serves as accommodation for any happening that would attract a large crowd, has been up to now the best place to enjoy sport on the island, but a new stadium is being built on the Claude Noel Highway outside Bacolet which is expected to regenerate all types of sport in Tobago. However, there should still be no problem in your participating in a game of beach or street football if you're so inclined.

| 8 |
Tobago's art scene

The art movement

Edward Hernandez, curator of the Tobago Museum and a well-known artist, affirms that he was in his earlier years part of the art movement which took place in Tobago in the 1960s. 'Tobagonians,' he says, 'had always been interested in the visual arts but puritanical views of ungodliness related to art and the portrayal of the human form had held sway from the earliest of times. Tobago was at the time and still is to some extent a very unsophisticated, highly religious society.' As a boy he remembers being chastised by his grandparents for drawing people and for always wanting to reproduce something on paper. Far from being admired, folk art was seen as a desecration and not really encouraged. Yet there were those who persisted.

When the 1960s came though, all art forms got off the ground with a bang. The celebration of national independence for Trinidad and Tobago was the spur. The Tobago Art Group was formed, and the movement to interest people and teach and practise all forms of art got under way, spearheaded by a strong-minded Tobago woman, Eileen Armstrong Guillaume, who must be considered the godmother of the foundation of the arts in Tobago.

Every sphere of society which could be involved, was. The public library too was caught up in the action and became the venue for meetings and art classes for teachers and others who, it was planned, would first master the art forms, then go on to teach their charges.

It was, apparently, a small renaissance. Vidia Naipaul, a famous Trinidadian novelist, visited and held talks, and musicians, pianists and others from the world of arts also came to make their contribution at this exciting time. Artists earlier regarded as naïve or primitive were now more politely called 'Heritage' artists. Drumming came out of the remote country villages and began to be enjoyed and regarded possessively as 'we ting'. The nation had been given a mandate by the Prime Minister of the period, the Honourable Dr Eric Williams, to demonstrate its artistic ability and it set to with a will. Tobago was determined not to be left behind. All the excitement and planning that was taking place in Trinidad generated waves of equal strength in Tobago as well.

Singing and drumming

Singing and drumming are the oldest expressions of art in Tobago, the drum itself having been, in all likelihood, the first musical instrument ever made on the island. The early Africans brought to the island carried within themselves the memory of the instrument and its significance in their lives, and there was plenty of virgin wood available. The drum has been at the basis of artistic and religious expression from the earliest beginnings of Tobago society, and today there are many shapes, sizes and tones of drums and many famous exponents of the art of drumming on the island.

Tobagonians have even added another dimension to drumming in the form of the tambrin drum (short, no doubt, for tambourine). This is a different, small drum about 18 inches (45 cm) in diameter and five or six inches (12-15 cm) deep, created, some think, so that it could be easily hidden from 'Massa', since drumming itself was definitely outlawed for much of the period of slavery. The tambrin has its own peculiarly light but resonant sound and is an excellent accompaniment to the fiddle which is used in the reel and jig particularly, and generally whenever a tune sets up.

Steel drums (DONALD NAUSBAUM)

Over in Black Rock, Malcolm Melville is an expert drummer and maker of drums, including the tambrin. His drums are taken all over the world by people who are fascinated by them and by the seeming effortlessness of his play. No doubt they realise quite quickly that it's not as easy as it seems.

Art centres and galleries

The excitement of Independence is long past but it encouraged a whole new way of thinking about art which has remained. Now there are wayside painters and carvers, mainly in the areas frequented by tourists it's true, but at least they're present. There was an Art Centre at Fort St George, Scarborough, where the works of local artists were shown, but this was closed for renovation a few years ago and is still (2002) being restored. Yet the art movement is still alive – not kicking very much and with no home, but definitely still alive.

The Art Centre is a temporarily closed door but the permanently open windows which have appeared on the scene are the new art galleries displaying the works of Tobagonian and Trinidadian artists, and these are very impressive indeed. One, simply called **The Art Gallery**, is located at Hampden, Lowlands. Simplicity, however, ends with its name. Set in a delightfully wooded area with a stream attractively overgrown with waterlilies, this gallery's location is in itself a showpiece. The owners are Martin and Rachael Superville and much of the work that they show is their own, but they also carry the works of well-known Trinidadians such as Jackie Hinkson, Sundiata, Lisa O'Connor and Jean Albert, and Tobagonians Jason Nedd and Jenny Hilton Clarke. They demand a high standard.

Both Rachael and Martin work mainly in oils and Martin has specialised in painting Tobago's women engaged in their day-to-day activities – washing at a stream, dancing, gardening, taking care of children. Both produce studies in rich, vibrant colours, which have considerable appeal.

The gallery is planned to be not just a formal display centre for works of art but a place where one can relax, have a cup of tea or glass of wine, paint if so inclined or simply enjoy the tranquil surroundings. There's a small shop at Crown Point as well, selling smaller art pieces and special cards.

Over at Grafton, directly overlooking Stone Haven Bay, Maureen Meyer at **Jungle Art** shows the work of aspiring local artists in a

Some of Louise Kimme's sculptures at her home near Mount Irvine (MIKE TOY)

variety of media. She insists upon high-quality, individualistic work and there are many fine pieces on display including wood carvings, carved and painted calabashes, leather, beadwork and beautifully carved and threaded drums. Her mission is to support and encourage local artists as much as possible. Also displayed is her own work in watercolour and painting on silk, which is both delicate and dramatic. All the pieces are carefully displayed to their greatest advantage and Maureen makes use of local props such as driftwood, sea fans and shells. It's an excellent locality, easily accessible and near to two major hotels, the Grafton and Le Grand Courland, and there's an absolutely fantastic panoramic view of Stone Haven Bay (Grafton). Jungle Art also offers painting vacations for those who may wish to dabble a bit while enjoying Tobago's sea and sun.

Louise Kimme, a German sculptress, spends most of her year on the island at her studio **Fairyhaus** on the border of Bethel village just

Local craftwork *opposite* (DONALD NAUSBAUM)

The Cotton House Batik Studio, Bacolet (MIKE TOY)

above Mount Irvine Golf Course. Kimme specialises in sculpting entire tree trunks into long, graceful, life-sized figures, representing the population around her; she portrays men, women and children engaged in everyday activities. Her work is unique on the island and her studio is well worth a visit.

At the grassroots level, craftwork is accessible on the streets and along popular beachfronts such as Store Bay, Mount Irvine, Stone Haven Bay and Great Courland. You can find tie-dye and batik cloth and clothing, and exotically painted jerseys and wraps depicting rain-forests, parrots, fish and other wildlife. Store Bay has a craft market with numerous booths, although variety here lies essentially in the quality of the work rather than in the design, as most sellers tend to offer the same types of goods. Some of the jewellery made from shells and beads is quite attractive. One can also get basketwork and crocheted items, and the Blind Welfare Office out in Bacolet also sells these. Special shops such as **Cotton House**, Bacolet, and **Backyard** at Crown Point offer clothing designed from high-quality batik and tie-dye material.

A craft market at Store Bay (MIKE TOY)

Street art

The street art of itinerant vendors is available throughout the island and although much of the carving is quite roughly done and not truly original in concept, it can be attractive and worth buying, especially some of the African-style masks and wall hangings.

Garvin Barrow, popularly known as the **Bull Horn Man**, gives a unique dimension to carving. In a small workroom barely six feet (2 m) square under his house on Government House Road, where the tools of his trade hang neatly on hooks or nails in the wall and a comfortably padded chair establishes his work position opposite the upside-down tub of a discarded washing machine used for visitor seating, he produces the most delicate and dramatic masterpieces of horn art.

This artistic side of Tobago's beef industry makes use of the horns of bison, cows, bulls and goats. Goat horns are used only for special items or are simply polished, decorated and hung as they are. The horn is softer than others and almost translucent, so polishing gives it a truly lovely finish.

A display of carved horn and other local crafts (DONALD NAUSBAUM)

The horn of each animal is unique in colour shape and size, but apparently cows provide more beautiful horns than bulls. All of them, however, are quite dull before the first polishing, which reveals the true colour of the horn. The Bull Horn Man studies a horn after polishing and sees in it the form he must create. He then proceeds to carve whatever creature has spoken to him, be it fish, bird, or animal. His bananaquits and armadillos, dolphin and black grackle are extremely popular items. You'll catch him at any beach, quietly selling his creatures from the sack slung over his shoulders; a quiet man this, but when it comes to his art, he has a wicked way with a blade.

| PART III |

The environment

| 9 |
Eco-Tobago

In a world that is fast deteriorating ecologically, Tobago stands as one of the last bastions of the naturalist. Its rich natural system displays an amazing variety of plants, birds, insects, coral and other aquatic life which, because of the size of the island, exists at really close quarters to human beings, making it virtually impossible for one not to notice and be enthralled. In case you're wondering about the proximity of aquatic life: in the shallow waters all around the island it's quite common to be suddenly overtaken while swimming by schools of tiny sardines which pass over and about, tickling bathers as they go.

Tobago's Forest Reserve is the oldest in the western hemisphere and represents the original natural vegetation of the island when it slipped away from the South American mainland some 11 000 years ago. As a result of that ancient connection, much of its plant and animal life has derived from the teeming natural life of the southern continent. As far as the Main Ridge Forest Reserve is concerned there is much to be thankful for in the fact that instead of being cut down to make way for sugar cane in 1765, a decision was taken for its protection, reserving it to the British Crown and thereby ensuring a good rainfall for the island. This has been the most ecologically sound administrative decision that Tobago has ever known, for it is this centuries-old Main Ridge Forest that has continued to protect Tobago's environment not only by securing the rainfall, but also by providing a haven for various species of wildlife.

The birds have it!

Of all this wildlife, birds are the most visible - 210 species in all. From tiny little birds to large birds - from the hummingbird to the magnificent frigatebird - they are definitely on the scene. This may be because Tobago, apart from having its own resident varieties, is in the path of those birds migrating both north and south on their annual pilgrimages, so she gets a number of visitors as well. Whatever the

Cocrico *opposite* (DONALD NAUSBAUM)

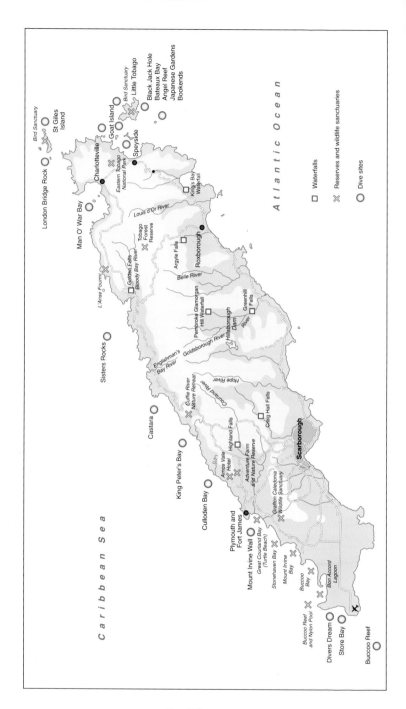

Eco-Tobago

Wooded ridge in the Central Rainforest Reserve (MIKE TOY)

cause, gardens all over the island are alive with birdsong every day of the year. The grounds of hotels and private houses, vegetable gardens, flower gardens and the roadside see constant bird activity, some of which can be quite amusing, like the antics of the black-faced grass quit, which is more or less always engaged in takinsg seeds off grass at the roadside but also entertains by jumping into the air at frequent intervals to look around and attract any passing female!

Frequent garden visitors like bananaquits, tanagers, motmots, mockingbirds, woodpeckers and doves have no objection whatsoever to being fed. As a matter of fact bananaquits and tanagers are particularly fond of brown sugar crystals, and the bananquit is also called the 'sucrier' because of its partiality to this food. Named because of its yellow and black banana markings, this tiny bird, oddly enough, does not seem to care so much for bananas, although a very ripe fruit will be eaten because of its sweetness. But it's amazing to see the quantity of sugar these creatures can tuck away in a day. As many of them as can hold onto the rim of a dangling, sawn-off, dried coconut shell filled

91

with brown sugar will perch there to eat, until their persistent activity sends the shell and them spinning around and around. They don't hop off until the sugar's all gone, either!

The motmot, or the king of the woods as it's called in Tobago, loves scorpions, cockroaches, centipedes and cheese. These are fantastic-looking birds, with a brilliant blue and turquoise crown, orange breast and long, central tail feathers with tips like racquets, which they swing from side to side like the pendulum of a clock. The bird always seems to be biding time! But it keeps a sharp eye out for cheese and will come regularly to a feeding place. It will even take the food right out of your hand.

Bird enthusiasts in Tobago need a bird book for identification of species, because often, particularly in the countryside, there are delightful surprises just around the next bend. For example, as you go through Arnos Vale, especially near the water wheel, there are likely to be motmots on trees near the roadside, surveying your vehicle and you with proud eyes.

Motmot (RICHARD FFRENCH)

One of many good birding sites on the island is the tea terrace at the **Arnos Vale Hotel**. This hotel feeds its resident birds at tea-time and for guests this is a major attraction. The gong sounds, booming over the estate, and with a flurry of feathers, with chirps and calls, they come sailing in for tea, expecting a double share most of the time – yours and theirs! An intimate experience this, and one well worth having.

Grafton Caledonia Bird and Wildlife Sanctuary is perhaps the best place for birding in all Tobago. Grafton Estate has always been famous for its birds, particularly its cheese-from-the-hand-eating motmots. As a wildlife sanctuary it was the brainchild of Eleanor Alefounder, the owner of the estate, who inherited from her husband, Peter. Mrs Alefounder recognised in 1963 that in the wake of destruction left by Hurricane Flora, the habitats of birds on the island, including those at Grafton, had suffered greatly, causing considerable competition for the food sources that remained. She started feeding the hungry birds every day, thereby forging the first link in the chain of daily feeding that Grafton would continue.

Bananaquits at Grafton Caledonia Wildlife Sanctuary, Black Rock (MIKE TOY)

Blue-gray tanager (DONALD NAUSBAUM)

Once the bird feeding programme had started, the verandah at Grafton House was soon frequented by cocricos (rufous-vented chachalaca), king of the woods (motmot), varieties of tanagers, bananaquits, tropical mockingbirds, woodpeckers and many other types of birds; taxi drivers soon began taking visitors there to enjoy the spectacle.

On her death in 1983, Mrs Alefounder left much of the land in trust, with the wish that her favourite tenants - the birds - be well looked after. So Grafton's trustees continue the tradition of cracked corn, bread and cheese, every day at four o'clock.

The Sanctuary is a non-profit making organisation, so there is no charge for viewing the birds or exploring the many forest trails in search of other wildlife. Grafton House, where the original feeding started, though separate from the Sanctuary, is available for rent. Modernised it has been, but the old architecture remains and the ambiance is still wonderful. Most importantly, the wildlife know that Grafton is theirs and they behave as proprietors do!

The **Bon Accord Lagoon** near Pigeon Point is a wildfowl sanctuary where one can find ducks, egrets and herons as well as a variety of other creatures. This is a good place to visit with a tour guide or on your own.

Easterfield Road in Mason Hall and Menna Trace, as well as **Cuffie River Nature Retreat** off the Moriah Road, which has a small hotel built to fit unobtrusively into its forest surroundings, are excellent places to find the elusive blue-backed manakin, the collared trogon, and Tobago's range of dazzling hummingbirds such as the white-tailed sabrewing (which had suffered in the hurricane but seems to be gradually re-establishing itself), the black-throated and green-throated mango, the ruby topaz hummingbird, the copper-rumped humming-bird and others. At Cuffie River there are nature trails to follow and the opportunity of meeting some forest inhabitants such as the tattoo, manicou, iguana, agouti and gorgeously hued snakes as well.

Beyond Charlotteville there is an old road to **L'Anse Fourmi** – now dangerous for vehicular traffic but a very rewarding hike affording intimate views of considerable bird and animal life. This is a good place to spot cocricos in their natural habitat.

The rufous-vented chachalaca or cocrico is Tobago's national bird, and its cry is as impressive as its name. This large but not particularly attractive bird has the features of a pheasant, and can be quite a pest in fruit or vegetable orchards. Having been at one time protected, its numbers increased to such proportions that it was proclaimed an agricultural pest, and there is now open season on it once more.

The cocrico loves to squawk in the early hours of the morning, giving a wake-up call that can be heard for miles around.

The beautiful, dramatic offshore islands of **St Giles** and **Little Tobago** are home to large families of Atlantic seabirds. There is the magnificent frigatebird, which can be seen in great numbers every day flying up and down the windward coast, always high up in the sky riding the thermals. The frigatebird is a very impressive creature which can have a wingspan of as much as seven feet (2 m) or more. It never rests, or does not seem to, for it takes its food from the ocean or from other birds on the wing. There is a story that a long time ago the pelican stole the frigatebird's beak; now the latter is always trying to get it back, hence the constant mid-air raids.

Little Tobago is also called Bird of Paradise Island, because years ago a colony of birds of paradise had been introduced there and had thrived beautifully. Unfortunately Hurricane Flora put an end to this.

ST GILES ROCKS

The St Giles Rocks, also known as the 'Melvills', were once part of the Charlotteville Estate, but around 1968 were presented by the owner of that estate to the Government of Trinidad and Tobago for the establishment of a wildlife sanctuary. St Giles Island, just about half a mile (1 km) off the north-east coast of Tobago, is the largest of these rocks, and has become a significant breeding ground for Caribbean seabirds. There are noddies and terns, brown boobies, red-footed boobies, red-billed and white tropicbirds and of course frigatebirds, as well as many other species of seabirds. Every day in Tobago, one can see numerous frigatebirds beating up or cruising down the Windward coast on their way to or from St Giles.

Magnificent frigatebird (RICHARD FFRENCH)

However the island continues to provide refuge for a unique cross-section of bird species, encouraging scientists and birdwatchers to flock to this bird sanctuary from all over the world to study or simply enjoy boobies, brown pelicans, gulls and the exotic red-billed tropicbird, which soars and glides in its display. It's possible to get very close to the nests of this white beauty, which are on the ground or in the branches of dense bushes, in March and April, when the chicks are still in. No one is allowed to visit Little Tobago without a guide.

Butterflies, lizards, frogs and snakes ...

But birds are not Tobago's only forte in the ecological stakes. Despite her size, she has a variety of habitats to encourage animal life, and her tropical rainforest, mangrove swamps and open savannahs, while not very extensive, support an interesting and impressive range of creatures. Apart from her 210 species of birds, there are 23 different butterflies, including the spectacular blue emperor, which ranges local forests, savannahs and gardens. As far as lizards go, there are about 16 different types including the sally painter and the undisputed beauty, the entrancing, bright green iguana, which lives on fruits and is often seen strolling across a lawn, its long tail fully extended like a majestic train.

That loud but not unmusical clamour in the evening emits from the throats of at least 14 kinds of frogs and there are no fewer than 17 types of bats, one of which is a confirmed night fisherman, in the sea of all places. Snakes number about 24 different kinds, none of which are in the least poisonous, but are indeed beneficial since they are the sworn enemies of rats. To this variety of creatures add mammals such as the tattoo (armadillo), agouti, manicou (opossum), quenk (collared peccary), red squirrel, and the caiman or small alligator, which prefers to bask in the sun and not trouble humans but is a serious predator in rivers and streams among crayfish. Other sealife includes fish such as the guppy, and crabs, among which is the manicou crab, so named in Tobago because it carries its young in a pouch.

Turtles in Tobago!

Perhaps the most remarkable creature that you can see in Tobago is the leatherback turtle.

Turtles have been on the earth for millions and millions of years, before even the dinosaurs. Yet today extinction threatens all the species that still exist, especially those that nest in the Caribbean Sea where according to old fishermen, they used to be more numerous and definitely larger than they are today.

The scientific name of the leatherback turtle is *Dermochelys coriacea*, the skin turtle, but in Tobago it is called by other names as well such as 'caldon', 'coffinback', 'balatie' and 'torti a cles'.

On any night from March to September a walk on the beach at Great Courland Bay (Turtle Beach), Englishman's Bay, Bloody Bay, Parlatuvier, King Peter's Bay or even Goldsborough or Bacolet could offer the spectacular sight of a leatherback sea turtle laying its eggs in the sand.

These giant, soft-shelled turtles can weigh up to 2000 pounds (900 kg) and although they live in cooler latitudes of the United States, Canada and the eastern Atlantic Ocean, they travel to the Caribbean to nest because their home grounds are far too cold to serve as

Leatherback turtle (CORBIS)

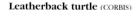

nesting grounds. They need the warmth of the Caribbean sun, so these islands offer warmer temperatures and to all appearances ideal nesting conditions.

But the islands also offer destruction, for many of the leatherbacks are killed when they come ashore to lay their eggs. Their predators never stop to think that not only the turtle but her eggs too are lost when she is killed, and as a result the turtle population is in steady decline despite being protected by law. Each female must lay thousands of eggs in order that her species may survive, but only a few hatchlings in a thousand will survive to maturity and lay eggs of their own.

Leatherbacks, the largest of the sea turtles, feed almost completely on jellyfish, having a particular palate for that highly poisonous creature the Portuguese man o' war and being totally immune to the poison of these jellyfish which causes human beings so much pain and suffering upon contact.

Very thick layers of fat keep leatherbacks warm and they are therefore able to survive in extremely cold water. They also dive very deeply and research has shown that females nesting in the Caribbean can dive to depths exceeding 4000 feet (1 200 m).

Once mature, female leatherbacks perform the amazing feat of returning to the beaches of their birth every two to five years, laden with eggs. The temperature of the sand in which the eggs incubate determines the sex of the hatchlings. Warmer temperatures produce female turtles, and males result from colder temperatures. Once hatched, the baby turtles break through the sand and head for the sea, a short but perilous distance away because of the seabirds that are always on the lookout for vulnerable prey. Even in the water the life of a baby turtle is very precarious, for many predatory creatures and other dangers await it.

Watching a female leatherback come up from the ocean to lay her eggs is an amazing and memorable experience. One moment there's nothing at the water's edge except the waves, monotonously breaking, and then suddenly she is there. She is huge, sometimes easily six feet (2 m) long, and has no shell, only a thick skin covering her back. She is totally focused. At this point the hawksbill turtle can easily be deterred by lights or noise, but the leatherback seems locked into the ritual that

Protected bay at Blue Waters Inn, north of Speyside *following pages* (MIKE TOY)

she must perform and most of the time will come steadily on, making her way slowly up the beach, searching for a spot, always high above the watermark, in an area of loose sand that pleases her. In the water she is the fastest turtle alive, but once on the beach she moves very slowly.

Having located her spot she starts digging, measuring the depth of her hole intermittently with her flippers, her eyes streaming mucous 'tears' that expel the salt from her body and at the same time protect her eyes from the sand flying energetically off her flippers as she digs. She does not concern herself at all with people who may be around her. When she is satisfied with the depth of the hole she stops digging and starts to lay her eggs. When she has finished laying, she carefully fills the hole with sand, covering the eggs completely and moves off to another area to create a diversion. This she does by making marks on the sand, describing large circles that could lead searchers away from the place where she has laid her eggs.

Finally, her task done, she heads for the sea again. The ocean accepts her as easily and as noiselessly as it had given her up and her great body disappears, leaving one to wonder how many of her hatchlings will, in their time, caught by the same impulse, return to the beach of their birth.

This compulsive fidelity on the part of the leatherback and the frequency with which sightings occur on Tobago's beaches have spurred such general interest that private citizens and special organisations such as Environment Tobago arrange turtle watches, and hotels keep their guests advised of the dates and times.

Environment Tobago

Environment Tobago (ET) was launched in February 1996. Its mission is to 'conserve Tobago's natural and living resources and to advance the knowledge and understanding of such resources, their wise and sustainable use and their essential relationship to human health and the quality of life.'

Some of Tobago's coastal waters are at times contaminated and through the Tobago Community Water Watch Network, ET has been monitoring the island's near-shore waters, rivers and storm drains in several coastal communities to determine sources of sewage pollution. A report of these findings was published in 1999 and there is now a pilot project in progress to develop design criteria for onsite sewage treatment and disposal systems suited to Tobago's varying environmental conditions. Phase one of the project has been started at Charlotteville.

ET has been advocating the need for a scientific study of flora and fauna population levels on and around Tobago and to this end is facilitating a pilot survey of Little Tobago Island. This data would help ET to lobby for the establishment of protected areas, as well as provide a baseline on which to gauge future changes in the population levels of Tobago's flora and fauna. Researchers from several universities have been recruited to conduct the survey. The vegetation and small mammal surveys have been compiled and other surveys are under way.

ET also keeps itself informed of developments and activities which may be harmful to the environment and in an effort to reduce the effects of such activities, informs the public of them and initiates discussions with those responsible. As a result ET is invited to take part in developmental discussions and to have representation on various committees which have an impact upon the environment, such as the Committee for Conservation Tourism Project, the Task Force to Prepare a National Biodiversity Strategy and Action Plan, and the Environment Committee of the Tobago Chapter of the Trinidad and Tobago Hotel and Tourism Association.

A comprehensive environmental education programme for Tobago is being developed by Environment Tobago and there is a strong lobby to have environmental education integrated in the new curriculum being designed for the primary schools of Trinidad and Tobago.

(Courtesy Environment Tobago. Website: http://www.scsoft.de/et.)

| 10 |
Exploring inland waters: waterfalls and river walks

Hunting waterfalls in Tobago is a very rewarding venture. There are numerous falls, some of which are easy to reach, while others involve longish walks, perhaps in riverbeds or along stony banks, and yet others demand considerable enterprise, energy and determination because of the terrain - usually mountainous and almost vertical - in which they are located.

Even for the accessible ones like Argyle Falls, it's best to go with someone who knows the way, and for the more difficult a qualified guide, such as Mark Puddy of Scarborough, is definitely necessary. Forestry Division or reputable tour guides are best able to give advice on these excursions.

The immediate advantage of seeking out waterfalls is that they afford a great opportunity to commune with nature in a very intimate way. Tobago is excellent for this. Some may even find that nature gets a bit too intimate! Walking up a riverbed flanked by towering trees and high bush at very close range can be a bit daunting, but the important thing to remember is that in Tobago it's very, very safe. The few snakes that there are in Tobago are definitely non-poisonous and all of the other creatures, except the mosquito, are more likely to avoid you than to come looking. The mosquito, however, has to be catered for and repellent does the trick!

Creatures apart though, that distant sound of water plummeting from a great height is undeniably exciting, and enchantment lurks in shady places of deep green ferns and bamboos swaying gently over the river like the giant fans of some spectacular eastern potentate, while sunlit clearings where brightness has managed to break through the greenery entice one to linger.

The island's tropical woodlands are alive with bird and insect life, providing a delightful variety of jungle noises. Mattiemamselles - dragon-

Argyle Falls on the windward coast *opposite* (MIKE TOY)

flies – dart and skim over the surface of the rivers, their delicate, gauze-like wings glittering in the sunlight. Butterflies and moths are in evidence everywhere. Many rivers, such as the Moriah, have small falls or rapids running through rocky areas – refreshing places for water massages – and long pools deep enough for swimming in the clear water. Local opinion varies as to whether river water is cool, cold or warm, but those from colder climes will most probably think it warm!

Despite the fact that Tobago is a small island with relatively short rivers, her waterfalls are clean. There are no pesticides, no fertiliser or waste of any kind except forest humus which is inevitable. Most rivers lend themselves to walking in their shallower parts. The Goldsborough River for instance, which leads one to the beautiful Rainbow Falls, is quite wide at some points, particularly nearer to the sea, and can have caiman – small alligators – but these bask in the sun and never attack, leaving the largest predator around in the water to be the crayfish,

Reservoir at the Hillsborough Dam, 100 feet (30 m) above sea level, with a storage capacity of 225 million gallons. This is the largest and most reliable source of potable water in Tobago. (MIKE TOY)

106

which sometimes reaches the size of a large prawn and has the added charm of being highly edible. So there really is nothing to worry those who would swim or wade.

In order to get to falls and rivers one passes through various types of terrain. In some areas it's an old cocoa estate. The cocoa trees are still there and many of them are bearing, for the island derives some income from cocoa, but wherever the cocoa trees are, so too are the stately immortelles which have sheltered them from the sun for all the years of their growth.

On the windward side of the island, heading out to country, as Tobagonians would say, there is the **Hope River**, with rapids and falls and pools deep enough for enjoyment even if not for actual swimming. Hope itself has a rather beautiful beach – long, wide with hard-packed sand, good for walking, running or doing tai chi. The sea itself is dangerous though, having very bad currents and frequent, perilous rip tides. Folks usually say that only people from Hope know how and when to bathe in the sea there.

Starting at the sea's end of the **Mount St George River**, which is just a short way from Hope, there is a series of rapids and deep pools and finally a largish waterfall with a very deep pool that is certainly suitable for jumping and diving. Further upstream this river are the remains of an old sugar mill, and the coppers – ultra-large iron pots which were used for boiling the sugar – can still be seen. The crushing plant for the canes and the remains of the old water wheel are there as well, but are difficult to spot, being covered by trees and high bush which have sprouted unchecked over time. This really is a worthwhile visit and not at all difficult to manage.

Further along the Windward Road is **Goldsborough River**. There are several falls on this river which are worth seeing. The first one, **Rainbow Falls**, is on private land and you may have to pay the owner a fee to guide you there. After parking the car, there's a walk of about a three-quarters of a mile (1 km) along a natural trail which leads through an area where magnificent bamboos, gently murmuring as only bamboos can, arch high overhead, forming a spectacular tunnel called the 'Cathedral' because it is so awe-inspiring.

This is butterfly and bird territory. There are motmots, oropendolas (yellowtails), jacamars, raucous parrots and chachalacas, kingfishers, woodpeckers, hummingbirds galore, and of course tanagers and bananaquits. Water sparkles over a sometimes stony, sometimes sandy bed with crabs, river lobster, mullet and the odd caiman. It's flat going all the way to the falls, sometimes through pleasant groves of banana trees, and a fruit orchard with mango, avocado, citrus trees and even sugar cane plants.

The fall itself, standing out against large boulders and the peripheral green of surrounding plants which are kept vital by its fine, constant spray, plummets into a wide, deep basin (good for swimming) and is truly beautiful. As the sunlight glistens through this fine spray, it causes a prism effect of many colours shimmering in the sunlight – hence the name Rainbow Falls.

The **Argyle Falls** just before Roxborough are definitely worth a visit as well and organised tour guides are waiting to escort you. This is a very popular trip for there are many large, deep pools on the Argyle River that are good for swimming. The terrain through which Argyle runs is interesting too, being an old cocoa estate. This is a good river for adventure, very deep in places, with many huge boulders and demanding some agility. The crayfish should be sizeable too!

At Louis d'Or there's a plant nursery for the island and far inside at the back of the nursery runs the **Louis d'Or River** which has rapids and pools deep enough for swimming at this spot. Both adults and children enjoy this part of the river as well as the walk following its winding course under trees, which is very pleasant and relaxing.

Not too far away from Louis d'Or is the **King's Bay Waterfall**, just before the entrance to King's Bay itself. These falls used to be quite spectacular, and still are to some extent, but most of the water at the source above has been diverted to other areas to supplement the village water supply, leaving the present fall rather thin. However, the atmosphere is relaxing, with trees and a gently gurgling stream, and if you can scale the large slippery rocks of the falls, there are pools at the top where you can at least get wet.

Highland Falls on the **Courland River** is reached from the Northside Road, as it passes through Mason Hall. This is a very challenging hike and a four-wheel drive is an absolute necessity here. This fall has the longest drop in Tobago, and it's supposed to be a thrilling experience to swim in a pool that is virtually on the edge of a 100-foot (30-m) waterfall!

Englishman's Bay River emerges on the beach, and the river walk leading from the beach upstream offers excellent wading. There are two tributaries, one of which takes you to a series of small falls. There

King's Bay Waterfall *opposite* (MIKE TOY)

are no swimming pools on this but the climb leads you right into Tobago's rainforest, and that's exciting in itself. There are largish falls on the other tributary but these are difficult to access. The bird life and flora in this area are exceptional, with motmots and jacamars being frequently seen.

One small fall, the **Golden Falls** on the **Bloody Bay River**, can be found quite easily by walking down Gilpin Trace from the Roxborough and Bloody Bay Road. This well-known trace actually leads into the rainforest.

There are other falls that can be explored, and local guides will know them. Guides should always be contacted, for what may seem on a map to be easy terrain may turn out to be difficult. Remember, distance is hardly ever a problem when hunting for falls in Tobago, but accessibility can be at times. Not very often though, and usually you forget all about the difficult climb when you arrive under that pounding torrent of sparkling water.

River and beach, King Peter's Bay (MIKE TOY)

| 11 |
Agriculture

Trinidad and Tobago are separated from each other by 21 miles (34 km) of ocean, but have been linked politically and economically for over a hundred years. Yet each island has its own very distinct character and contributes very differently to the national cultural landscape. Tobago is very rural, but because of its links to Trinidad its economy has been dominated since the 1950s by the Trinidad-based petroleum sector with its associated chemical (ammonia, methanol, urea) and steel manufacturing industries. This emphasis on oil and related industries, and the lure of the resulting industrial jobs and their greater rewards have been to the detriment of agriculture generally in both islands but in Tobago, where the population is smaller, their effect upon the labour population has been even greater. Indeed, agriculture in Tobago was recently estimated as contributing less than 2 per cent of the GDP, although many of the island's families have at least part-time interests in agricultural enterprises.

(PHOTO BY DONALD NAUSBAUM)

Much of the agricultural land is owned by the state, and even though some of that land was distributed years ago, a great deal of it has not been used productively. The last agricultural census for the nation in 1982 revealed that there are about 30 000 agricultural holdings in both islands, of which at least 2000 are in Tobago. But of this 2000, only a small proportion are believed to be commercial enterprises.

Fruit and vegetable production in Tobago is aimed only at the island's fresh market and at the hospitality industry, which has been developing steadily with small and medium concerns and now has one very large resort in the development stage and others planned. One of the disadvantages for Tobago of its union with Trinidad is that because inter-island trading is unrestricted, for both these markets – the local fresh and hospitality – Tobago farmers face serious competition from Trinidad farmers, who have a greater land area for planting and can produce their food at relatively low costs compared to their Tobago counterparts.

The advantage for Tobago however is that in contrast to Trinidad where there is a high use of agricultural chemicals in production, farming systems in Tobago are generally low input, with few or no chemicals used; this is attractive to the hospitality industry, whose patrons tend to be very aware of chemical hazards. Also, the island has been developing cottage-type enterprises, using its local crops to produce a wide variety of high-quality processed goods such as pepper sauce, green seasoning, preserved fruits, jams, pickles and confectionery, and is becoming increasingly expert and professional in packaging and marketing these items; they have done very well both at the national level and in the wider Caribbean market.

All of this is achieved with the help and encouragement of the Tobago House of Assembly, which since its establishment in 1980 has made serious attempts to arrest the decline of Tobago's agricultural output. The Assembly, with the assistance of other national agencies such as the Agricultural Development Bank, the Small Business Development Corporation and the Tourism and Industrial Development Company (which also support farmers and agro-processing in both islands), has involved itself in every aspect of Tobago's agriculture, not least in research into the development of products such as bay oil, plantain chips and local flours. It also supports the Tobago Industrial Cottages at Goldsborough, Roxborough and Speyside, which produce 'Taste of Tobago' products.

This thrust by the THA is based on its development plan for Tobago, which recognises that in view of the modernisation and development of agriculture in Trinidad, Tobago, being far smaller, can never recapture her once enviable reputation of being the food basket of the nation; however, she can still move from dependent consumption into productive self-reliance and feed, if not the nation, at least herself.

A good plan this certainly is, but many factors have got in the way of its realisation. Topography and poor soil conditions make a large part of the island unsuitable for cultivation. Steep mountain slopes are dramatic and beautiful, but their use for agriculture is severely limited because of erosion and poor accessibility. What arable land remains in this little paradise is in small pockets on the coastal plains and in the valleys. Only in the south-west (a very popular tourist location) where the land is flatter is there potential for intensive agriculture. But here tourism is a serious competitor for land space. Some land that could be used for agriculture lies deserted as state land or abandoned estates, and other land again has been diverted to non-agricultural uses.

Then, of course, there's the people problem. In today's world, even in Tobago, farming is not a popular occupation. Labour is usually provided by the farmer and his family and is mainly a part-time activity. Even where it's not, the complaint is that reliable labour is both scarce and costly and few enterprises are large enough to hire labour full-time.

Lend-hand, one of the inherited African co-operation customs whereby farmers or anyone else in need of labour may help each other as required, still exists and eases the strain in very particular circumstances, but labour is still a problem. The disdain which was linked to the plantation agricultural system of the colonial period remains – to the extent that farmers themselves do not even want their children to 'inherit the land', so to speak, and become farmers. As a result the farming population is ageing, and for young people, working in agriculture tends to be a last resort if one can't get anything better to do, rather than a planned career.

Yet Tobago manages to get some of the job done. The available land is rich and not overworked, and there are food crops of which the island can boast such as pigeon peas, plantains, breadfruit, cassava, watermelon, tomatoes. These are the traditional crops that the Tobago farmer has always grown and they are well known nationwide, but nowadays farmers are also being encouraged to grow cantaloupes,

Guavas (DONALD NAUSBAUM)

pineapples, sesame and beet, both for the tourist industry and for local consumption.

Fruit is particularly plentiful in these islands, with something in season all year round. There are mangoes, sapodillas, grapefruits, oranges and mandarins; bananas, papaws, pineapples and watermelons; also chennet, peewah, soursop, sugar apple and pomerac as well as pomme-cy-there, five finger, mammee apple, star apple, cashew, guava, coconut and a variety of plums.

Top favourite is the mango. We who live here may dispute varieties, but the popularity of the fruit remains constant. The mango is juicy, sweet, succulent, even erotic, and comes in many shapes, sizes, textures and flavours, all capable of bringing delight.

Papaw or papaya, known long ago as breakfast melon, is everyone's standby. Never out of season, it is the fruit of a tree that grows all over Tobago. The tree has a tall, erect stem, with an umbrella-shaped crown under which the papaws grow in very close clusters. The male papaw tree does not fruit, but its graceful tendrils of flowers serve to pollinate the female. The fruit is long or oval, green when unripe and yellow or pinkish when ripe. Inside, the firm flesh surrounds a mass of small seeds that are usually discarded because of their laxative effect. Squeeze a lime over it, and enjoy the flavour!

The citrus parade is also very impressive. In the dry season grape-fruits, pink-fleshed and otherwise, compete with sweet-as-sugar oranges and brilliantly coloured mandarins, portugals and tangerines, themselves sweet with a delightful tang. Then there's the shaddock from which one must remove a large wad of skin before coming to the fruit. But it's worth the trouble! The skin of the shaddock is often used to make slices of a candied peel sold by confectionery vendors.

Sugar loaf is not only the name of a mountain in Rio de Janeiro, it's also the name of a pineapple which grows right in Tobago. Not in very large amounts it's true, but we're getting there. The sapodilla? Well, that's to die for! Picked green, it's washed in salted or sea water, and put to ripen. When they're ready for eating you'll smell them.

There are also special large and small estate crops such as coconut and cocoa and some root crop Tobago specialities including yam, dasheen, eddo, cassava and sweet potato, together with legumes (the pigeon pea is world famous) and vegetables - pumpkin, tomato, christophene, bodi, and so on.

Livestock development on the island has generally shifted towards small ruminants rather than large animals and with the assistance of the Caribbean Agricultural Research and Development Institute, familiarly called CARDI, techniques have improved and more animals are available to farmers, making Tobago a major player in the effort being made to reduce the country's dependence on imports of mutton from New Zealand and Australia.

It's a small island and grazing is a problem, so the livestock, particularly the beef cattle, graze primarily under the coconut trees and at the roadsides, but they do thrive, and hair sheep and goats are widely cultivated for the meat market, many of them going to the Trinidad market. Pigs make a hearty contribution to the local meat sector and there are also a few rabbit, chicken and duck producers.

The beekeeping sector is very active, with about 30 beekeepers holding 600 colonies of bees, and the island is fast becoming well known for its honey. Tobago takes advantage of its mite-disease- and Africanised-bee-free status to produce a glorious multi-floral honey,

Coconut plantation, Shirvan *following pages* (MIKE TOY)

which has so far won 24 awards over the last ten years at the prestigious National Honey Show in London. As well as honey bees there is also the indigenous sting-less bee, the object of collaborative research with the University of Utrecht.

The Tobago House of Assembly looks after its farmers through a range of agricultural stations. The main agricultural office for crops is at the Botanic Gardens in Scarborough, but there is also one at Goldsborough, while Louis d'Or's nurseries supply ornamental plants, vegetable seedlings and fruit tree plants. Two breeding units are located at Runnemede and Charlotteville, and livestock demonstration takes place at Louis d'Or and Hope.

The THA is also responsible for plant quarantine services, monitoring the airport, yachts and the Post Office to protect local griculture from potential pest and disease problems being brought into the country. Through its Department of Natural Reserves and Environment it sees to the reafforestation of watersheds and other areas, the management of National Parks, and wildlife and environmental management. At Studley Park there is a forestry nursery which produces forest species such as mahogany, cypre and cedar, popular woods for furniture in the island.

Animal health services cover veterinary provision and there are livestock stations such as Blenheim Sheep Multiplication and Research Project and stations at Hope Farm, Louis d'Or, Kendal, Charlotteville and Runnemede which serve as demonstration stations and also supply stock to farmers.

In the area of fisheries the Department of Marine Affairs and Fisheries keeps the register of fishermen and boats and sees to reef management. It also monitors the many fish-processing plants, supervises data collection on fish, and trains people under the recommended international standards.

Fisheries resources in the waters around the island are very high, particularly in deep-sea areas. There is evidence of this in the fact that fishermen come from Barbados and Trinidad to fish the waters. These resources are supported by the island's position on the continental shelf of the north-eastern part of South America and by several reef formations that surround it, yielding such fish as dolphin, tuna, shark, albacore, snapper, kingfish, bonito, salmon, jacks, wahoo, cavalli, salmon, flying fish and others, all of which, apart from supplying food for the nation, facilitate an exciting Carib International Fishing Competition each year.

CARIB BEER INTERNATIONAL
GAME FISHING TOURNAMENT

The Carib Beer International Game Fishing Tournament, sponsored by Carib Beer of Trinidad and Tobago and organised by the Trinidad and Tobago Game Fishing Association, has taken place in the April of each year since 1981, at Pigeon Point on the south-east coast of Tobago. The year 2000 saw its twentieth anniversary celebration.

In 1999 there were 183 anglers and 37 boats from Europe, Great Britain, the USA, Canada, Australia and the Caribbean to participate in the event, competing for over $325,000 in prize money, plus the chance to win a motor car.

This is a very laid-back, competitive but not anxious three days of fishing in the Caribbean Sea, with a lay day for relaxation, fun, getting to know each other and exchanging the inevitable fishing tales.

Technology is present but not obtrusive. The radio control, opting for originality, is manned from a thatched shed under the graceful coconut palms on Pigeon Point, with its antenna fixed in a coconut tree.

Eligible species of fish are the blue marlin, white marlin, sailfish, yellow-fin tuna, dolphin and wahoo, and the usual size of these creatures of the deep has created considerable spectator interest in the sport, so many locals and visitors flock to the bay to have a good look.

However, the organisers, with an eye to protecting species which may be endangered, have started awarding 350 points for releasing fish instead of bringing them in. In 1999 an angler who bagged a 644-pound (295-kg) fish broke the blue marlin record! What a long tale that must have made!

The fishing methods of the local fishermen include trolling and banking and the use of nets and lures. Seemingly casual, this fishing industry has traditionally been an important activity in Tobago, providing the main economic support for many coastal villages. There are approximately 28 landing beaches in Tobago regularly used by 850 registered fishermen, and some of these have storage facilities for nets and equipment, changing rooms and pipe-borne water for cleaning and gutting fish and washing down.

Helping to pull in a seine on a beach is a good way to get in touch with the local fishing population in the villages. This exercise takes place regularly, and extra hands on the ropes are always welcomed. Castara is a good place for this, and it's an education to see the real colours of the fish as they emerge flapping from the water.

Generally speaking, the future looks bright for all aspects of agriculture in Tobago. Tourism itself is seen as a major developmental factor. Instead of allowing its agriculture and tourism sectors to tug against each other because of the land space that each needs to develop, the island is making a concerted effort to join the two in the enterprise of *putting Tobago first*. It is determined to forge a strong link between its tourism drive and its agricultural development, recognising that while quantity of output is a desirable agricultural goal, emphasis must remain on supplying a high-quality final product with minimal chemical residue, using only environmentally friendly technology.

Fishing boats at dusk, Grand Courland Bay (MIKE TOY)

| 12 |
Off the deep end in Tobago

Tobago's water world is fascinating. Whether you indulge in only the gentlest of snorkelling activities over shallow reefs such as Buccoo or Store Bay, or prefer stimulating deep-sea diving, aiming for heart-pounding drift dives, canyon walls, reefs teeming with fish and being in close, exciting contact with manta rays, this small island, caught between the Caribbean Sea and the Atlantic Ocean and near enough to South America to enjoy the benefits of nutrients generously transported by the Guyana Current from the mighty Orinoco River, offers everything below the waves that could possibly be desired.

Diving

Dive sites are numerous, some of course being more exciting than others, but each has something special to offer. There's London Bridge, Bookends, Flying Manta, the Japanese Gardens, Black Jack Hole, the Sisters, Mount Irvine Wall, Culloden Bay, Buccoo Reef and others. Interested in coral particularly? There are 44 species under Tobago's waves of both hard and soft coral, as well as one of the world's largest brain corals which is 12 feet high by 16 feet across (3.5 by 5 m) and still growing off Speyside.

The nutrients bestowed by the Guyana Current attract large pelagic creatures such as rays, mantas, dolphins, sharks, tarpon and turtles to inhabit the island's plankton-rich water which, by the way, has a very high degree of visibility at depth, happily exposing to view all of these undersea wonders. Water temperature averages around 24°C (75°F).

Some of the best diving in Tobago is to be had at the north-eastern end of the island, around the offshore islands of St Giles, Goat Island and Little Tobago, which are off Speyside.

London Bridge, which goes down to a depth of 110 feet (33 m), is an extremely rewarding dive for skilled divers, but can be dangerous. It is a natural rock shaped like an arch, or perhaps more like the arched back of some prehistoric monster rising from the deep. (Not

Into the deep blue; a snorkelling excursion from a pirogue (MIKE TOY)

THE STORY OF BUCCOO REEF

Cecil Anthony was a famous reef diver and boat operator of Tobago. His name is synonymous with Buccoo Reef and he earned for himself the title of 'King of the Reef'. He and Sullivan Dillon were the first reef operators to provide visitors to the reef with diving masks, opening up the underwater world to their delighted eyes.

The reef saw its first visitors in the 1930s. They were from England and their main pleasure at the time was being able to walk on the reef flats and collect lobster, conch and whelks. At that time, Tobagonians regarded the reef mainly as a source of food, so it is no wonder that this was the aspect of it to which they introduced their visitors.

Then, one day in the 1940s, the inevitable happened. One Mr Slaney brought the first diving mask to Buccoo, with the intention of making diving for conch and lobster easier. Suddenly, not only could visitors see the lobster and

122

Glass-bottomed boat *Solo Amor* on Buccoo Reef (MIKE TOY)

conch clearly, they could also see the reef itself and the beauty of it hit them very forcefully. Making their view of that beautiful underwater world available to tourists seriously occupied their minds. Soon another mask appeared as a gift from 'an aunt in the USA'.

Dillon and Anthony proved themselves to be very inventive young men. They made a glass box that enabled visitors to view the reef and its colourful inhabitants from inside the boat! This was the beginning of the era of the glass-bottomed boat. Anthony went on to import diving masks from Jamaica, and to become famous for his trick of catching nurse sharks with his bare hands. He and Dillon were the first reef operators to provide their guests with masks to view the reef, in the late 1940s.

They did not keep the monopoly for long, however, for masks became available in Trinidad in the 1950s and were soon common among operators. When the competition became too strong at Buccoo, some of the operators started doing business from the area around Swallows and Pigeon Point. The first true glass-bottomed boat appeared, captained by a David Johnson and operating out of Bon Accord Lagoon, in 1965. It started doing business on the reef but its visits were confined to the Nylon Pool, then known as Dance Bank, and the Sea Gardens for the display of coral, sea fans and fish.

Hurricane Flora in 1963 did considerable damage to the reef and because of this and the fact that operators had been encouraging their customers to walk on the reef, it became necessary for the authorities to establish some sort of control. A reef patrol officer and boat were introduced to protect the reef, and Dr Goreau, a renowned ecologist from the University of the West Indies, carried out a study of Buccoo.

The 1970s brought the Marine Areas Preservation and Enhancement Act and a Marine Area Order, which designated Buccoo Reef as a restricted area and forbade the removal of flora and fauna. The number of glass-bottomed boats increased however, and reef operators, despite the law, continued to encourage people to walk on the reef. Three additional reef patrol officers were appointed, a new boat was acquired and the Institute of Marine Affairs, on behalf of the Tobago House of Assembly, did an ecological survey of the reef. The 1990s brought a further arrangement between the THA and the Institute of Marine Affairs to initiate a Coral Reefs Project, which would include the management of Buccoo Reef.

Today it is illegal to remove anything from the reef; it is now absolutely vital to protect that valuable but delicate ecosystem.

a very heartening analogy if one is intending to dive, but there it is!) In this dive one can see snapper, spotted moray, sea whips, golden crinoids, large colonies of star coral and colourful sea sponges.

The coral reef around **Little Tobago** is very highly rated by divers because of the variety of creatures, including mantas, that are found there. Dive operators boast that this is a diving adventure found nowhere else in the Caribbean. They claim that as you descend to the reef, giant mantas totally unafraid of you, some with massive wingspans, dance a ballet of welcome to their world. It is reported that in time the mantas get to know their visitors and permit them piggyback rides through the undersea world, earning for themselves the affectionate sobriquet of 'Tobago taxis'. Just the same, dive operators, out of concern for the mantas, do not normally encourage this practice.

Over in the Caribbean the **Sisters Rocks** offer very good diving too. Angel fish abound and the rocks themselves are covered with beautiful coral. **Mount Irvine Wall**, also in the Caribbean, is well known for its

The Sisters Rocks (MIKE TOY)

night-time displays of octopuses, lobster and orange ball anemones. In 1977 whale sharks, the largest fish in the world, suddenly appeared at **Divers Dream**, a dive location in the Caribbean, three or four miles (4-6 km) off Pigeon Point. Two of these peaceful creatures that feed on small fish and other tiny animals were encountered by a group of divers. This caused much excitement in the diving world and the whale sharks have obliged by returning twice a year! They are also seen now quite regularly off St Giles and even off Little Tobago.

Diving is mainly done off the small pirogues manned by island boatmen who know their business well, but glass-bottomed boats convey those who prefer to admire the ocean's depths from a more secure position above the waves, to take a snorkeller's view of such wonders as the **Angel Reef** (named after the numerous varieties of angel fish that inhabit it), the **Japanese Gardens** and the famous **Buccoo Reef**. From Speyside village these boats make a stop at Goat Island to permit their passengers a lengthy, comfortable snorkel among hamlets, rock beauties, blue tang, parrot fish and others, then off they head for the largest brain coral in the world.

125

Until recently, Tobago had no wreck dives. One would think that with all the battles fought in bays around the island, there would have been wrecks at reachable depths to be explored, but none have been found; the sea has done a thorough clean-up job, and what is not totally covered by 300 years of silt has long since broken up. Those were the days of wooden ships, after all.

In 1997 Keith Darwin of Aquamarine Dive in Tobago and Reginald McClean, with the co-operation of TIDCO, Trinidad and Tobago's Tourism and Industrial Development Company, and the Association of Tobago Dive Operators, established a wreck dive site in 100 feet (30 m) of water on a sandy bottom just a quarter of a mile (0.5 km) off Mount Irvine Bay on the Caribbean coast.

The wreck is, appropriately, that of an old inter-island ferry – the *Scarlet Ibis* – which for many years made the daily run between Trinidad and Tobago, transporting people, goods, vehicles and everything else. She had been renamed the *Maverick* after being sold by the government and it is as the **Maverick** that she rests at the bottom of the Caribbean Sea, having been donated for the enterprise by Coastal Diving.

She was sunk not just to manufacture more undersea excitement, but with the ecological aim of reducing the impact on Mount Irvine Wall by giving divers another dive option in the area. It is said that every dive on a reef has some deleterious effect on it, even if only a small one.

The *Maverick* is in an upright position facing north, and the experiment is proving a success. The vessel has become a home for reef fish and pelagic fish as well, and is now completely covered in Atlantic oysters, which seem to have found the environment they needed. Sea cucumbers and coral have also made the *Maverick* their home, and brick structures have been added (by her human developers) to accommodate smaller creatures such as shrimp and crabs.

This ambitious venture has turned out so excellently that the Dive Operators Association is contemplating repeating the exercise with another boat off Speyside.

Snorkelling

Apart from its diving sites, Tobago also caters for the snorkeller who does not want to go far out into very deep water. Just off Mount Irvine Beach – the part known as Mount Irvine Public Beach – there's an interesting reef, very good for snorkelling, with a wide variety of fish, strangely shaped rocks and large sea fans moving in the tide.

Mount Irvine Bay Watersports Shop, Mount Irvine Bay

There are parrot fish and eels, triggerfish, grunts and butterfly fish and one sometimes sees the odd red fish or grouper

Buccoo Reef, the old-time favourite for snorkellers, has suffered because of its accessibility as the sea there can, at low tide, be no more than knee-high. Unthinking visitors have taken its beautiful coral and sea fans as souvenirs of their trip, and this has damaged the reef, but its ten acres of coral gardens are still extremely beautiful and well populated with fish, crabs, eels, and so on. Glass-bottomed boats make many trips daily to Buccoo from either Buccoo village, Store Bay, Pigeon Point or Mount Irvine and after the reef visit they stop at the **Nylon Pool**, which is a natural shallow area of clear water in the middle of the ocean, where one can swim in safety and comfort.

Other places where snorkelling is easy and exciting are at Black Rock, Plymouth Back Bay, Store Bay, Castara Small Bay and Englishman's Bay. These are all easy to reach and no guides are necessary. Being able to swim, though, is absolutely essential. There is much to see. The sea

Dusk on board Kalina Cats' charter catamaran *Ocean Spirit* (MIKE TOY)

does not give up all her secrets, but she gives a little hint here and another there of the wonders of the underwater world. You might suddenly be exposed to a rush of sardines, darting here and there in the water, more concerned about your appearance in their habitat than engaged in any exercise to drive you wild. Then there's the sand fish, sand-coloured and almost impossible to see because of its perfect camouflage - which it does not seem to trust, because it darts off in a panic if you get close. It's a quiet, beautiful, beguiling world under the sea, but it is important to remember never to go alone and always to stay alert.

Sailing

Tobago's sea adventure does not stay under the waves, and lovers of wind and surf will find plenty of watersports on offer. Well-organised specialist companies arrange Hoby Cat (catamaran) sailing trips to Castara, Englishman's Bay, Charlotteville and around the 'cape of Tobago' to Speyside. There are also mini-safaris with overnight camping at chosen bays and charters on live-aboard sailing yachts. The 'cats' are fast and with the wind behind them on the Atlantic coast can make the trip from Speyside to Pigeon Point in less than four hours. They are 16-footers (5 m), best described as sailing dinghies with two hulls, and

Clear water and coral heads, Buccoo Reef (MIKE TOY)

they offer a view of the island very different from that gained in a vehicle or from the air.

Most of the leisure cruise companies offer romantic sunset or moonlight sails with cocktails and food included. There is nothing to beat a tropical sunset unless it's a full moon hanging low over the ocean, and these cruises are truly out of the ordinary; they are also very relaxing, putting you in just the right mood for the next day.

ANGOSTURA YACHTING WORLD REGATTA, TOBAGO

The Angostura Yachting World Regatta hosted by the Trinidad and Tobago Yachting Association is an annual regatta that runs in May for one week and includes the first-day opening ceremony, final-day prize giving and a lay day.

Yachting World magazine has dubbed this 'the friendliest Regatta in the Caribbean', and rightly so, for it is a combination of competitive, heady racing between Crown Point and Grafton and exciting fun events which add up to a memorable week.

Now in its eighteenth year, the regatta takes place off the south-west coast of Tobago, where vigorous currents and steady winds add an exhilarating dimension to the already keen racing atmosphere. It attracts local, Caribbean and foreign sailors alike, racing up-to-the-moment-technology spinnakers, designed for the greatest speed. Not only are the boats in this class highly efficient, but their crews, tacticians and skippers are shrewd and sharp. In the cruising class, racer cruisers also have their experienced crews and skippers, every bit as keen as in the spinnaker class, and the competition is definitely as fierce.

Then there's charter racing and comfort cruises – again non-spinnaker classes – the latter apparently taking along the whole family, the kitchen sink and the family pets.

Yachts come from more than 15 countries to this regatta, yet the friendliness of the event persists. It retains the warmth and spontaneity that are Trinidad and Tobago's national characteristics. All possible facilities are provided and each year a jetty is specially constructed for the convenience of participants going ashore, while Regatta Village, set up at Crown Point Beach Hotel, is an ideal meeting place for after-race activities.

Lay day – the laying up of the boats for a day – takes place at Pigeon Point and is a recess from the daily school of racing, but it can't really be considered a rest day because there's too much activity going on. Visitors, locals and participants have the opportunity to mingle in the far less competitive atmosphere of bailing water from boats contests, ball games and beach racing, with a bit of goat racing thrown in.

There's music, of course and dancing. Drinking action? What sailors' lime is without it? And fun? Definitely!

BUMBOATS

The bumboat or fisherman's boat is a work boat as distinct from a pleasure craft, used mainly for setting seine, carrying cargo, etc. and you can see them at these tasks every day. They have been traditionally sailed at regattas held over the Easter weekend and were used by local sailors racing against each other long before the outboard motor entered the picture.

In the 1950s and '60s, when fishermen from other islands such as St Vincent, Bequia and Carriacou sailed down to Tobago to fish, races between the visitors and locals became popular. The tradition has continued on Tobago's windward coast where bumboats are still built and the increasing popularity of regattas in the Caribbean has given the bumboat the opportunity to show what it can do.

Their owners are fiercely proud of them and are willing to compete against yachts to show off their boats' prowess. The chance to do this comes during the Angostura Yachting World Regatta, but over the Whitsun weekend as well these colourful boats hold the sea-stage with no intrusions from other craft. They are the traditional boats of Tobago, and the fierce pride of the Tobago fisherman in the beauty and capability of his boat, the work she does to make his living and the heritage that comes with her will keep the bumboats going to sea for many a year to come.

(PHOTO BY MICHAEL BOURNE)

| PART IV |

Touring the island

| 13 |
The Caribbean coast: Crown Point to Arnos Vale

Store Bay at Crown Point is the starting point of this section of the Caribbean coast tour from Crown Point to Plymouth and Arnos Vale, a good afternoon's excursion since it's not very far. The second leg of the tour follows the Northside Road from Scarborough to Mason Hall and Moriah all the way up to Parlatuvier, then down to Roxborough on the Windward Road, and is best done as a full day's tour.

Store Bay is easily the most famous and popular of all of Tobago's beaches, highly appreciated for its clear waters and fine, white sand that is very firm underfoot in the water. The snorkelling is also very good, for there's a small but rewarding little reef with a variety of fish and other creatures.

Generally the sea is quite calm, but as is to be expected there are times, at Easter for instance, when things can get very rough indeed and lifeguards have to be particularly attentive. Even at its roughest though, Store Bay is a magnificent - or perhaps one should say an awesome - sight that can be enjoyed from a safe distance, just so long as you're not in the water when that thunder and surf scenario is taking place!

This bay has the added advantage of being very near to the airport. It's an easy walk across, even with baggage, so visitors tend to have a last dip in that glorious water rather close to departure time, or a first dip as soon as they arrive, particularly if they are staying at one of the many hotels and guesthouses that are just a few minutes' walk from the beach. Numerous car rental and bike services in the area make it quite easy to become mobile in a hurry and if a sky trip is desired, there's always the helicopter service.

Another good feature is the new beach facility with small shops, bars and snug little cook shops, where every day some of Tobago's best cooks of Creole cuisine serve their exotic concoctions, such as

Ocean Spirit **under sail** *opposite* (MIKE TOY)

Caribbean Sea

Englishman'

Castara Bay Casta

Mount
Dillon

King Peter's Bay

Runnemede

Moriah

Culloden Bay

Courland River

Golden
Lane

Les
Coteaux

Arnos Vale

Mason
Hall

Belmont

Plymouth

Fort James

Concordia

Adelphi

*Great Courland
Bay*

Providence

The Whim

*Stone Haven
Bay*

Black Rock

Mesopotamia

Fort Monck

Claude Noel
Highway

Hope

*Mount Irvine
Bay*

Mount Irvine

Patience Hill

*Hillsborc
Bay*

Booby Point

Scarborough

*Buccoo
Bay*

Buccoo

Bethel

John Dial

Minister Poir

Pigeon
Point

Prospect

*Rockly
Bay*

Fort
King
George

Bacolet

*Minister
Bay*

Lambeau

Shirvan

*Store
Bay*

Canaan

Mount
Pleasant

Bon Accord

*Little Rockly
Bay*

Fort
Milford

Lowlands

Crown
Point

*Canoe
Bay*

*Columbus
Point*

Tobago

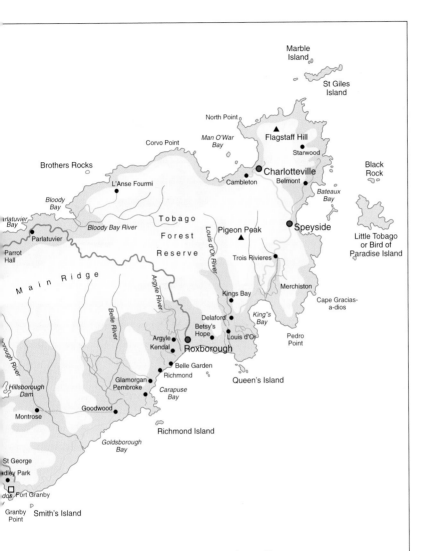

Marble
Island

St Giles
Island

North Point

Man O'War
Bay

Corvo Point

Flagstaff Hill ▲

Starwood

Brothers Rocks

Black
Rock

L'Anse Fourmi

Charlotteville

Cambleton   Belmont

Bateaux
Bay

Bloody
Bay

arlatuvier
Bay

Tobago

Bloody Bay River

Forest

Parlatuvier

Reserve

Pigeon Peak ▲

Speyside

Little Tobago
or Bird of
Paradise Island

Parrot
Hall

Trois Rivieres

M a i n   R i d g e

Argyle River

Belle River

Merchiston

Cape Gracias-
a-dios

Kings Bay

Delaford

Betsy's
Hope

King"s
Bay

Argyle

Kendal

Louis d'Or

Roxborough

Pedro
Point

rough River

Belle Garden

Richmond

Queen's Island

Hillsborough
Dam

Glamorgan
Pembroke

Carapuse
Bay

Goodwood

Montrose

Richmond Island

Goldsborough
Bay

St George

dley Park

dos Port Granby

Granby
Point   Smith's Island

Atlantic   Ocean

CRUSOE'S CAVE, CROWN POINT

This cave is located on the extreme south-west tip of Tobago on the Atlantic coast. The best directions for finding it are: 'behind the airport, down the road from National Petroleum'. Anyone in that area will direct you. Its name is, of course, a direct allusion to Daniel Defoe's character, Robinson Crusoe, for Tobago is rumoured to have been Crusoe's island.

Crusoe's cave is part of a network of subterranean caves that traverses the Crown Point and Store Bay area, and is thought to have been a prehistoric fresh watercourse used by the Amerindians who occupied that part of the island.

---

curried crab and dumplings, coo-coo with callaloo and fried fish, stewed conchs, stewed chicken with red beans and a mouthwatering variety of other gourmet dishes.

The series of forts along Tobago's Caribbean coast starts here at Crown Point with **Fort Milford**, a small but very pleasant fort on high ground just south of Store Bay, which affords a long, beautiful coastal view of that part of the island, with stands of coconut trees (referred to on the island as 'coconut wharfs'), the Nylon Pool out in the Caribbean Sea and Buccoo Reef not far away from that.

Built by the British in 1777, Milford was used by the French after they captured the island in 1781 until the British reclaimed it in 1793. However, between 1642 and 1660, before either British or French came, there used to be a Couronian settlement and a Dutch redoubt named 'Belleviste' in the area. In 1777 during the course of the American War of Independence, an American privateer, Oliver Cromwell, raided the coast but did not succeed in taking the fort.

The arrangement of Fort Milford is very interesting. Six cannons, five British and one French, are mounted on a raised semicircular platform which is protected at its outer limit by six formidable bastions of coral stone, in an arrangement quite unlike that of any other fort on the island. The walls of the bastions, each being about two feet wide and six feet high (0.6 by 1.8 m), must have afforded very good protection to the gunners operating in the spaces between them. The bastions themselves face north directly on to Store Bay, strategically placed for its defence.

The grounds, though not extensive, have a good display of purple bougainvillea and red ixora, and there is an old-fashioned turnstile and

Fort Milford (DONALD NAUSBAUM)

circular paving stones leading to well-worn benches under shady almond trees. On the southern side of the fort is Milford Bay, where in olden times ships loaded up with the hogsheads of sugar and perhaps kegs of rum that had come in from neighbouring estates.

Pigeon Point, a short distance from Store Bay, is another popular area for bathing and relaxation. It's a wide expanse of land that used to be part of the Bon Accord Estate, an old coconut plantation that also includes the Bon Accord Lagoon. It has a long beach of white sand, very similar to Store Bay, and turquoise water that is hardly ever ruffled. It also has a romantic jetty or pier, on top of which there is a hut covered with coconut fronds. This pier is probably the most often photographed tie-up for boats in the world, and has appeared in numerous magazines and books.

The facilities at Pigeon Point - the bars and eating places, changing rooms, bathrooms, toilets and deckchairs - are all privately owned by the Aquatic Club which operates the place, so there is an entrance fee to the Point that covers the use of them, but one can use the beach and the sea without payment. That, after all, is the law of the

Pigeon Point, the most famous jetty in the world (MIKE TOY)

land. There is no objection either (for obvious reasons) to use of the bar or food shops.

This is a very popular spot with visitors and locals, including those from Trinidad. Every convenience is right here if you wish to spend the day, and people frequently do. Reef boats take off for the Nylon Pool and Buccoo Reef at regular intervals and there is sufficient food and drink at hand to satisfy a variety of tastes.

Believe it: when the sun is shining, the ocean is blue, and a balmy breeze ruffles the leaves of trees, Pigeon Point is as close to being a paradise as anywhere in the world is likely to get. It's a very safe beach for children. There is plenty of room for them to play, and supervision is virtually effortless from a deckchair strategically placed under a tree. Try to avoid a coconut tree though, for dry coconuts have a way of falling when you least expect them. However, it's likely that the trees here are regularly cleaned of dried nuts to prevent fallout.

Pigeon Point is the appointed base of the Carib Beer International Game Fishing Tournament and also the chosen 'lay day' venue for the Angostura Yachting World Regatta, both of which are extremely popular happenings on the island, drawing many of their spectators from the Caribbean as well as other parts of the world.

Bon Accord village and the **Bon Accord Lagoon** are on Milford Road, immediately after Pigeon Point. Part of the area, nearer the main road, is now given over to housing for locals and foreigners, but until a few years ago the entire place was more of a nature reserve, and the actual lagoon, which is in the area closest to the sea, supported a good assortment of birds, ducks, herons, crabs and other creatures, with no human competition. Now that most of the area has been filled in to provide house or business lots, the wildlife population has dwindled considerably.

However, the lagoon is still there, and even in other places, where houses have not yet been built, there is enough left of the old environment and vegetation to encourage crabs and other creatures such as herons. This a reasonably sure-fire spot to find the yellow-crowned night heron, which favours swamps, streams and places near the sea coast that can satisfy its mainly crustacean diet. The night heron is quite a large bird, with a hoarse 'quack' for a voice that one hardly ever hears because the owner seems always to be hunting and consequently stands absolutely still at a crab hole, intent upon that exit, making no sound but waiting with infinite patience for its designated dinner to emerge. It's a solitary bird, the yellow-crowned, diurnal in habit. They call it 'crabier' with good reason!

Another common resident of this wetland is the little blue heron, whose numbers increase during migration periods. Trinidad and Tobago are very well placed to benefit from bird migration, being on one of the main routes of migrants moving south down the Caribbean isles to escape the cold of the North American winter by wintering in South America, and of those coming from the south of South America – the opposite direction – to escape the southern winters. This is more true for Trinidad than for Tobago, but Tobago does manage to see a fair number of birds on their migratory passages. If you live here and are even just a bit observant it's easy to tell when they're in, because suddenly one day there are strange faces in the garden competing for food.

As well as two residents, the white-cheeked pintail duck and the black-bellied whistling duck, the lagoon also sees the green-winged teal, great blue herons, the great egret, little egret and the cattle egret, the last having adopted Tobago as one of its homes. In many parts of the island it is becoming a common sight to see a large number of cattle egrets roosting, in late evening, in a tree, transforming it regardless of its species into a thing of beauty; they seem like so many large white flowers just resting there, on a tree that one knows bears no flowers at all!

There are back roads in Bon Accord and Canaan which will take you to Buccoo village but it's best not to try to find them if you're unescorted; use the Shirvan Road instead.

Buccoo is very small, but famous for its reef and **Nylon Pool** out at sea. Boats can be hired here for reef tours or fishing trips as easily as at Store Bay or Pigeon Point, and there's an excellent beach that goes around to what's generally called No Man's Land, a favourite and idyllic picnic stop. Go there on a day when there are no barbecues and enjoy the absolute tranquillity. It's like being marooned on a deserted island, except that you are confident that the boatman will return.

Buccoo headland, reached by entering Buccoo village, affords a good view of Mount Irvine, Grafton and Black Rock. There's an interesting phenomenon visible from this point, which occurs among the waves

Tiny sandbar island off Buccoo Reef (MIKE TOY)

The **Sugar Mill** at Mount Irvine Bay Hotel, now adapted to form part of an attractive restaurant, was once the heart of operations at the Old Grange Estate when sugar was king. But the death of the industry sealed its fate and that of all the other mills in Tobago, leaving the estate to be planted in coconut trees in the early twentieth century.

The sugar mill incorporated into the restaurant at Mount Irvine Bay Hotel
(MICHAEL BOURNE)

near to the reef when the tide is high. The waves rush in together over the reef with high crests of foam running madly in the wind, like white-haired dancing dervishes or flying white horses whose manes are whipped by the breeze! Another good place to observe this is from Mount Irvine's Beau Rivage Restaurant, on a hill nearby in the hotel complex.

Sign at Mount Irvine beach (MICHAEL BOURNE)

Mount Irvine Bay Hotel and beach, **Stone Haven Bay** and Black Rock are along this route, as is the Grafton Caledonia Wildlife Sanctuary. **Fort Bennett** is a cosy little fort on a promontory between Stone Haven Bay (Grafton) and Great Courland Bay, drawing attention to the fact that forts along this coast, including Plymouth, have all been placed in positions which, when taken together, draw a net of protection across the coast that would have been difficult for any invader to break.

Fort Monck is situated on Rocky Point at the northern extremity of Mount Irvine Bay. It was established by the Courlanders in 1681 under the command of Colonel Franz Monck. By 1683 the settlement was abandoned, having been destroyed by Indians and disease. It is now known as Rocky Point.

The **Grafton Caledonia Wildlife Sanctuary** is the best wildlife sanctuary on the island and is particularly well known for its birds, especially its cheese-eating motmots that are willing to take this delicacy from your hand in one quick swoop. They are exquisite birds,

144

Black Rock Anglican church, old and new (MICHAEL BOURNE)

with an air of great intelligence, delightful to watch, very curious, and will regard you quite intently. The Sanctuary is also a good place to look for the blue-backed manakin; this is generally a difficult bird to catch sight of, but you may be lucky. Cocricos are there as well in full force, walking around the grounds, while the bananaquits are positively pampered by having bottles of sugar water hung out for their enjoyment. There are snakes too, as well as sally painter lizards and mammals such as the armadillo, but there are no poisonous snakes in Tobago and that's a comforting thought!

Black Rock is a friendly little village with small shops and two interesting churches. It's a good stop for a cold drink and fruit and a chat with villagers, since there are always people 'liming' around that area. It's small, so you get through it rather quickly but it has two restaurants, the Black Rock Café and Under D Mango Tree.

Black Rock Beach is small too, being at the northern end of Stone Haven Bay. Its sand is glistening black and the sea water totally transparent; the bathing here is excellent, with a small but lively snorkelling area. It's a

Painting at Black Rock Anglican church (MICHAEL BOURNE)

Stone Haven Bay, Black Rock *opposite* (MICHAEL BOURNE)

146

good place to see pelicans riding the moored fishing boats that are piled high with seines.

After Black Rock you begin travelling along **Great Courland Bay**, also known as Turtle Beach. Important historical events have taken place here and the name Courland commemorates the many attempts made by the Courlanders to settle Tobago, especially in this area. There has been much fighting between nations and it appears from the results of archaeological digs that the area also supported a reasonably large Amerindian population. This is a beach that's very well known

The Mystery Tombstone on the grave of Betty Stiven (MICHAEL BOURNE)

Fort James, Plymouth (MICHAEL BOURNE)

for sightings of the leatherback turtle. It's wide and very deep like a
large, round bowl, with lots and lots of that loose sand in which turtles
love to hide their eggs. It has an entrancing atmosphere on a moonlit
night too!

To get to Plymouth and Arnos Vale after this, one must cross the
Plymouth Bridge instead of going straight on to Les Coteaux. Plymouth
is the home of the Courland Monument, the Mystery Tombstone, Fort
James and the Lovers' Retreat Rock.

The legend on the **Mystery Tombstone** is an enigmatic one that
intrigues the thousands who visit each year. This is the grave of Betty
Stiven, who apparently died in 1783 when she was 23 years old. The
inscription on her stone says: 'She was a mother without knowing it,

Aerial view of the Fort James area, Plymouth *following pages* (MIKE TOY)

and a wife without letting her husband know it, except by her kind indulgences to him.'

The most popular interpretation of this statement is that Betty was the coloured concubine of a white planter who, caught in the rigid social conventions of his time, could not marry her regardless of the esteem in which he held her. She could however, have his children, and polite society would pretend that none of it was taking place. Whatever the explanation, Betty's story remains a mystery on which much speculation has been spent. Perhaps this is Tobago's oldest love story!

The **Courland Monument**, which lies on part of the site of the seventeenth-century Dutch-Courlander fortification – Fort Nievv Vlissingen/Jacobus/Beveren – is a monument to those old, adventurous, persistent Courlanders of Tobago's history. It was unveiled in 1976 during a cultural visit by Courlanders in exile, from different parts of the world. Every two years, coinciding with Tobago's Heritage Festival, these descendants assemble in Tobago for a reunion. Dressed in historic costumes of the period of their nation's early island adventures, they re-enact their landing at Courland Bay 300 years ago. The Monument itself represents freedom and was designed and built by one of Tobago's national artists, Janis Mintks.

Fort James, a short distance from the Mystery Tombstone, is the oldest fort site on the island. It is named after James, Duke of Courland, whose settlers were the first to occupy the area in 1650. From 1762, two companies of regiments were quartered nearby in thatched zhuts but by November 1770, when it was attacked by rebellious slaves, the site had been reduced to being a picket post manned by the British.

In 1777 the strength of the picket post was augmented by the addition of a four-gun battery of three 18-pounders and one six-pounder, manned by the militia and trusted slaves, who were called upon to do battle with the French in 1781. The fort itself was built around 1811 and permanent barracks for the troops were erected nearby as well, because apart from deterring invasion – always a threat in Tobago – shipping in Great Courland Bay had to be protected: this large, accommodating, deep-water harbour must have attracted trading ships and presented severe temptation to raiders in the Caribbean Sea.

Rugged coastline near Arnos Vale *opposite* (MIKE TOY)

The headland upon which Fort James stands is a beautiful one, commanding a spectacularly breathtaking view of Great Courland Bay, and it takes very little imagination to picture the scene as it was 200 years ago. To the north-west the wide, sweeping curve of the bay rises gradually into the hilly country of Whim, Les Coteaux and Providence and on a clear day one can see all the way over to Moriah and Mason Hall.

What remains of the original fortifications is a series of low walls built of cut coral limestone and faced volcanic stone with brickwork at their corners. There is also a separate bastion, built of the same material, but with an oval-shaped roof and a stout iron grid on the window. Four cannons, two of which are marked with the Tudor double rose and two with GR (George Rex), are positioned within the innermost wall, together with a powder magazine and an oven for heating shot, easily discerned by the mound of earth which served as their protection.

Lovers' Retreat Rock, Plymouth (MICHAEL BOURNE)

On the beach near Arnos Vale (MICHAEL BOURNE)

Arnos Vale Water Wheel (DONALD NAUSBAUM)

The grounds of the fort are very well kept. Green turf rolls down to the cliff's edge and the inevitable white picket fence that seems to feature at all the forts protects the unwary. There are spreading almond trees, mock immortelle and yellow cassia, and benches inviting you to linger in the evening, when the sun is setting over the Caribbean and Great Courland is alive with the late activity of boobies, pelicans, gulls and frigates making their last dives of the day.

Lovers' Retreat Rock is located off Rabbit Lane in Plymouth, and no one can explain why it has this name. It is a strikingly shaped arch of rock, off-white and dark brown in colour, which the sea has, over centuries, battered into shape. The scenery here is wild and exotic – a great place for a picnic and no doubt attractive to lovers.

From Plymouth to **Arnos Vale** is not far, and the road leads past the **Adventure Farm**, a good birdwatching spot with a pleasant garden. The area around the Arnos Vale Hotel is particularly charming, with numerous motmots to be seen. There is also an interesting water wheel and other machinery that used to be part of the estate's sugar mill works.

This is a good place to end your day's tour. The hotel offers a daily afternoon tea to visitors that its bird population cannot resist and you shouldn't either.

| 14 |
The Northside Road

The second leg of the Caribbean coast tour goes via the Northside Road, which begins in Scarborough at the junction of the Claude Noel Highway and the traffic lights on upper Wilson Road. It continues inland through some rather pretty villages for a bit, only coming close to the sea after Moriah and revealing many beautiful views of the Caribbean coastline from advantageous points high above sea level.

Having been built on a ridge, it's a winding road, twisting and turning from one village to the next, but with a reasonably good surface. It's already high up at its very beginning on the Claude Noel Highway, and it continues to climb, so by the time it gets to Concordia, which is not

Looking towards Castara from the Northside Road (MICHAEL BOURNE)

at all distant from your starting point, there is an unrivalled view of Scarborough, its port and all the surrounding areas.

Before Concordia, there's the section known as **Rockly Vale**, where the President's official Tobago residence is, but nothing of this can be seen from the road and there are armed guards.

The Northside Road cuts across the island from south to north in a north-easterly direction. The terrain through which it runs is very different from either the Windward Road or the Caribbean coast tour that started at Crown Point. Both of these have large stretches that are at sea level, but this is mountainous country where in places such as Moriah and Runnemede the land slopes sharply down from the road. One has to bear this in mind all the time and careful driving is essential, especially around bends, for there are many blind corners and it's important to keep to your own side of the road.

Except in areas where the natural land formation permits it, there is barely any verge on either side of the road. Many front gates, balconies of houses, entrances of shops and bars are right on the road itself, while the rest of the building is propped by high pillars rising from the slope or gully at the back. Because there are very few pavements, pedestrians are often walking on the road as well. Yet there is not a high accident record; in circumstances like these people are inclined to drive carefully.

At the **Providence** junction you must turn left off the Northside Road, and go into Providence proper. Villagers will direct you to the aqueduct which spans one of the tributaries of the Courland River, rising to about 100 feet (30 m) or more. It was built to bring in water for the sugar estate, but now stands forgotten, a silent monument to man's ingenuity.

The outer limits of **Mason Hall**, near the sign that says 'Welcome to Moriah', offer visitors their first view of an interesting little river which is quite easy to wade in during the dry season, but should not be attempted during the rainy season. The main pipeline for the Hillsborough reservoir, Tobago's largest source of drinking water, branches here to take some of its precious liquid to Government House Road and up to the service reservoir at Fort King George in Scarborough.

After Mason Hall comes **Moriah**, a village famous for its annual depiction in the Heritage Festival of an old-time Tobago wedding. The views are quite good around here, with many green slopes and valleys

Coastal view from Mount Dillon *opposite* (MIKE TOY)

and distant hilltops to admire. You are beginning to get near to the ocean when you see the sign for King Peter's Bay; King Peter was an Amerindian chieftain.

Over in Golden Lane, to the west of Moriah, is the grave of **Gang Gang Sara**, a slave woman who, centuries ago, was supposed to have flown from West Africa to Tobago, to take spiritual care of her people brought here as slaves. Legend has it that after Emancipation, with the slaves free, she decided to fly back to her homeland and attempted to do so by taking off from a high silk cotton tree. However, as she took off, she fell to the ground from this great height and died, because she had eaten salt during her sojourn in Tobago and had lost the power to fly.

Back on the Northside Road, at **Runnemede**, there's an ancient silk cotton tree - a huge tree, very tall with a massive base, evidence of the type of vegetation that made up the forests here in days gone by. Silk cotton trees have a special significance in Trinidad and Tobago, and perhaps in other Caribbean islands as well. Somehow they have become associated with the occult, or obeah, and people place offerings under them in an attempt to bring either good or evil, more likely the latter, to others. Whether it works is anyone's guess.

The beach at Castara Bay (MIKE TOY)

Englishman's Bay (MICHAEL BOURNE)

Around a bend leading out of Moriah one gets a first view of what used to be called the **Pagoda House**, a beautiful house with a roof like that of a Japanese pagoda, which was built by Parkinson, who used to be the Queen's photographer. He is dead now and the house, after being gutted by fire, was remodelled by its new owner, but people still refer to it as Mr Parkinson's house. The house nestles into a high hill that overlooks the Caribbean Sea and has a long-distance view of the hills and valleys all around it.

Shortly after the Pagoda House you begin the descent to **Castara** village. From the brow just above the bay it seems idyllic. Pirogues and sometimes small sailboats bob about on water that reflects the greenery from the land all around. The long, deeply curved beach of white sand is popular with nesting leatherback turtles and, as though Nature was not satisfied with her achievement, she made two beaches known, naturally, as Castara Small Bay and Castara Big Bay.

Parlatuvier Bay *following pages* (MIKE TOY)

The bathing is very good at Big Bay, and Small Bay, while not quite so good, has a reef that makes snorkelling there interesting. There are stingrays, barracuda, jacks, lobster, sardines and a host of small but very colourful reef fish, including the sand fish that camouflages itself by merging its colour so completely with the sand on which it rests that it is never discerned until one is right up to it, when it darts away.

Castara is also a very good place to spot sea birds. It is essentially a fishing village so pelicans, boobies, gulls, and frigatebirds are always around, constantly on the watch, surveying the sea for a tasty morsel. As the bay faces west, sunsets are highly visible and that great bowl of a sky comes alight with colour. On any given afternoon as the sun is setting, one is sure to see pelicans coming in on the horizon, very low over the water, their wingtips almost touching the waves; they seem not to be fishing but just having fun flying in formation, keeping in line to a beat that they alone can hear.

Seine-pulling takes place very frequently at Castara and this is an extremely interesting exercise in which you can participate if you wish. Also in Castara on a Thursday, in the yard of the Anglican School near the bay, village women sell the bread that they have baked in the old-fashioned clay ovens. Go early, for people come from far and wide to buy these loaves.

After Castara comes **Englishman's Bay** and its nature reserve. There's a short drive from the road down to the beach, through a wooded area with fascinating clumps of bamboo, large-leafed philodendrons, flowering balisier trees, hog plum and naked indian trees. Curious motmots and jacamars are here in quite large numbers, but are difficult to see because of the foliage. There's a stream as well, exiting at the far end of the bay, in which you can wade while admiring the lovely ferns. This is a pleasant beach for sunbathing, with a fairly large and efficient picnic area – encouragement to keep the party litter in one place.

Parlatuvier is next, a sleepy little village where nothing much happens except the daily trips by fishermen and children going to school. It's a bowl-shaped bay, as indeed they all are on this part of the coast, with a beach that grades steeply into the sea. This is nature's warning to be careful, because it indicates that your next step could be very deep indeed, causing loss of balance.

But Parlatuvier has a very charming attraction. The crested oropendola or yellowtail has brought fame to a stand of bamboo situated near the centre of the village, at the junction of Parlatuvier East and

Parlatuvier West rivers. The stand is known as the **Yellowtail Tree**. On any afternoon, for an hour or more before sunset, it certainly seems as though every yellowtail in the entire island is darting into that clump of bamboo to roost for the night. Hundreds of them obey this strange impulse every single evening, clucking and creating a great deal of activity and yet there are no nests, no young ones. Although this sleeping arrangement has been going on for the past 80 years, the yellowtails do not nest there and none of their long, graceful nests swing in the breeze to mark their overnight accommodation. They simply roost there: no one knows why.

Bloody Bay is so named because of a terrific battle that took place there, but now there are absolutely no reminders of it except the name. All is calm and peaceful.

Further up from Bloody Bay, at virtually the summit of the Main Ridge on which you have been travelling, there's a lookout which affords a dramatic view of the **Sisters Rocks** - a good dive location - and a wide expanse of blue Caribbean Sea. It's an excellent spot for

Bloody Bay (MIKE TOY)

taking photographs and stretching one's legs. There are female vendors at this lookout who are on the spot every day selling exotic concoctions of fruit drinks such as coconut and passion fruit, papaya and orange, Carib beer and tamarind. They also sell a variety of cakes and breads - banana bread, pone, fruitcake - all of them enticing and guaranteed to add a couple of ounces.

A little way up from the lookout you come to **Gilpin Trace**. If you're with a guide who knows the territory, and there's plenty of daylight left, by all means take a forest walk; otherwise leave this venture for another day when you can hire one of the many very efficient and experienced guides available.

The road is long and winding down to Roxborough on the Windward Road, on the other side of the ridge, but the surface is very good. The vegetation is a dense, thickly packed type of fern climbing up the hillsides or running along the ground, topped by tall trees including fruit trees, palms and the bois canoe, a tall, slim tree which has strange and very attractive multi-fingered leaves - they are often used in floral arrangements. There are not so many views here but it's a particularly pleasant drive. Just be careful on those curves.

| 15 |
Scarborough

Throughout the turbulent period of Tobago's history from around 1654, when the island was first settled by the Dutch, right up to 1814 when it was ceded to Britain, Scarborough has been the piece of ground most fought over.

Scarborough is Tobago's port. There is no other. No doubt its strategic location enhanced its popularity in the eyes of those who sought to take it and was one of the major reasons why the area was chosen as the capital of the island when Georgetown in Studley Park lost its status as such. Today, Scarborough is still the seat of the island's administration and the hub of all commerce and business activity as well.

There can be no doubt that this is an active, feisty little town that is easy to get around, particularly in a vehicle. It's also true that she can't be called charming as yet, and perhaps never will be, but she's definitely interesting. Right now she shows signs of having sprung hurriedly from the relaxed, 'whenever' business area that she used to be into the hustling, bustling centre of enterprise of today. The main area downtown, near the port, consists essentially of businesses - shops, stores, supermarkets, banks, eating places - a hive of activity during the day, especially on Fridays and Saturdays, for these are market and shopping days; but at night, after the *Panorama* (the inter-island ferry) has docked, Scarborough shuts down rather quickly, leaving open only some bars, restaurants, recreation spots and the island's one cinema.

The town is contained between the Claude Noel Highway to the north and the sea, Rockly Bay, to the south. Its main thoroughfares are Milford Road, Main, Carrington and Castries Streets and Wilson Road. Milford Road comes in from Lambeau and enters Scarborough by running alongside Rockly Bay and the sea wall, where some sort of esplanade is in the process of being built, to the port area where it becomes Carrington Street and then, further up, Castries Street, as it

Scarborough from Rockly Bay *following pages* (MIKE TOY)

starts the upward climb to Fort King George. Around the first bend, which, by the way, affords a great view of boats moored in the safe harbour, it becomes Main Street, joins Fort Street a little further up by the Methodist church, and continues up to Fort King George. Wilson Road runs north from the port, passing the market, the Electricity Commission and the Telephone Company, TSTT, then crosses the highway and continues out of the town.

Situated just across from Main Street, opposite James Park which is named after A.P.T. James, a popular Tobago politician, now deceased, is the rather beautiful building that houses the seat of administration in Tobago, the **Tobago House of Assembly**; it is a fine example of Georgian architecture.

Scarborough's residential area lies in this hilly part of town below the fort, but even here some businesses are beginning to intrude, because down on the flat it is very crowded. There are churches up here, Anglican, Roman Catholic and Methodist, with their attendant junior and secondary schools, and Scarborough Hospital, the only hospital on the island, is located at the top of the hill.

This is a very pleasant part of town, not at all restless or noisy, but with relaxed old houses, many of them very well kept, the homes of old Tobago families who have lived there for generations. In between these homes there are one or two genteel guesthouses such as **Hope Cottage** and **Mills Guesthouse**. These are well reputed from the days before tourism really caught on, when Tobago saw only a handful of regular visitors each year who were content to be cosseted in the comfortable atmosphere that these homes-away-from-home provided.

The route into lower Scarborough along Rockly Bay is very busy but scenic. The sea in Rockly Bay is rather shallow because of the reef out in the bay and the famous **Red Rock** that was at one time connected with the land but is now starkly alone out in the ocean, buffeted by the Atlantic. The relatively shallow water encourages gulls and pelicans to feed constantly and one can often hear their squabbling from the land. The ocean is always interesting here, inviting even, but it's not really good for bathing any more, as there is too much enterprise in the area and everything washes down into the bay. There was a time though, long past, when it was extremely popular.

The **Botanic Gardens**, off Gardenside Road, offer a different kind of scenery and relaxation. There are many interesting plants and trees, and also, because of the exalted position, good views of the surrounding terrain. (For further details, see p. 173.)

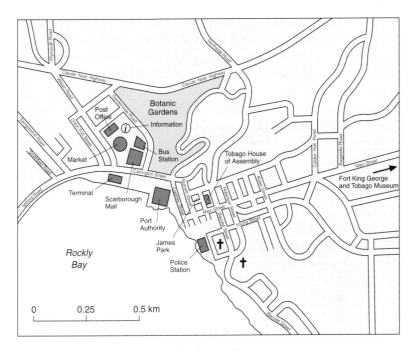

Scarborough

King's Well Inn, Scarborough (MIKE TOY)

Scarborough Methodist Church (DONALD NAUSBAUM)

Dockworkers' Recreation Club, Scarborough (MIKE TOY)

The Scarborough Mall, Post Office, market and library are located in the centre of town, easily accessible from each other, and the bus depot, from which buses leave to all parts of the island, is also in this general complex, on the Gardenside Road. There is another mall, referred to as the IDC (Industrial Development Corporation) Mall, but that is on Sangster Hill, off Milford Road.

THE BOTANIC GARDENS

The Botanic Gardens in Tobago are situated in the heart of Scarborough, which is ideal because a stroll through them at midday or in the late afternoon can do wonders to restore one's equilibrium.

The curator of the Trinidad Botanic Gardens, J. H. Hart, had first made the recommendation that gardens be established in Tobago and an attempt was made to construct gardens at the President's house, but these were not maintained. Approximately 18 acres of land of the Deal Fair Estate, owned by the sisters Miss Charity and Miss Scooby, were identified in 1898 as the new site for the gardens, but the sisters were not at all keen on accepting the Government's offer for their land, thinking it too low.

In 1889 the land dispute was settled when the courts awarded the sisters almost twice as much as the Government's offer, and the project went ahead rather quickly. Main drains, terraces, paths and bridges were laid down and a tool shed, nursery and the curator's residence were constructed.

Plants for the nursery were obtained on the local and the international market and their numbers increased so rapidly that sales were started in 1900. Trials were also conducted on a wide range of plants considered to have economic potential, such as amaranthus, arrowroot, chive, coffee, ginger and kola.

In 1914, administration of the Gardens was transferred from the Botanic Department to the Agricultural Department in Trinidad.

There are many beautiful flowering trees and shrubs in the Botanic Gardens, and Tobago has its own branch of a hard working horticultural society that is particularly concerned with its continued development.

The Botanic Gardens, Scarborough (MIKE TOY)

Scarborough market is open throughout the week, but only on market days are stalls piled high with produce - vegetables, ground provisions, cassava, plantains, breadfruit and a wide variety of fruits as well as meat, fish, spices, cocoa balls, plants. It is a colourful, vibrant place, with vendors in bright aprons and headties extolling the virtues of their wares and hailing customers.

Bacolet, another of Scarborough's residential areas, is really on the outskirts of the town, across Gun Bridge. Bacolet Street is a coast road, hugging the Atlantic rather closely; there is excellent bathing at Little Bacolet Bay. Bacolet Point and Bacolet Gardens are definitely up-market areas, with large homes, spacious grounds and an atmosphere of quiet gentility. **Fort King George** (see p. 176) is directly above Bacolet and at night the beam from the lighthouse probes the darkness of the Atlantic Ocean and stretches out over the waters to greet its sister light at Point Galera in Toco, Trinidad.

Bacolet Street connects eventually with the Claude Noel Highway, near the new stadium outside Scarborough.

Despite the fact that downtown Scarborough can be hot and dusty, particularly in the middle of the day, there is much native colour and excitement in the day-to-day activities of this little space. Fish vendors in their vans by the roadside blow on conch shells to attract customers

THE SNO-CONE

Sno-cone is a local ice delicacy which is popular with most people. It's an inexpensive way to beat the heat of a tropical day by having something cold and sweet. There must be variations of it in countries the world over. Children love it and adults do as well, because it's both tasty and refreshing. The sno-cone is shaved ice packed into a styrotex cup and drowned with a favourite home-made fruit syrup or mixture of syrups for which the vendor will never give the recipe.

Most customers clamour for guava syrup, made from ripe guavas, and the popular vendors like Scarborough's Mapio and his wife, who ply their trade on the town's streets, have other varieties of syrup such as tamarind and lime as well. The carts used by the vendors are insulated to protect the ice that must be carried around to make the cones. These carts are mounted on a sort of bicycle frame with either two or three wheels, which serves as transportation for both the vendor and his material; but they are heavy, so pushed carts aren't as mobile as carts which can be ridden like a bike.

Mapio rides a bike, but his wife doesn't. She pushes, and so is not able to get around as much as he does. Just the same, between them they cover the town very thoroughly and are extremely popular, answering to many a friendly shout of 'Oye, Mapio' during the course of a day.

In the old days, sno-cone was called snowball, because the ice was shaved with an iron shaver which packed it into a ball while it was being shaved, and that ball of ice was then dipped, by hand, into the syrup. The more modern arrangement of having a machine to grind the ice and a large bottle with a pump to put on the syrup is infinitely more sanitary, but just as popular! Pouring on a good dollop of condensed milk can jazz up a sno-cone, and this too is a favourite.

Fort King George, Scarborough (MIKE TOY)

and call out the names of their catch - red snapper, king fish, grouper, jacks - favourites of the Tobagonian palate; trucks from hardware stores, laden with bricks, rolls of wire, cement or sand, trundle along causing traffic blocks; drivers of route taxis call for passengers to Plymouth, Store Bay, Buccoo; and sno-cone vendors (the most popular being Mapio) blow their whistles or ring their bells in an attempt to coerce customers into purchasing their cooling concoctions. All of these activities are the life of the town, the very pulse of Tobago itself.

Fort King George

Fort King George in Scarborough stands 452 feet (138 m) above sea level - head and shoulders over the town, so to speak. This, the largest and most imposing of Tobago's forts, must also have been the most important because of its position and the wide area that it commands.

Its history has been almost as chequered as that of the island itself, for despite the fact that it was the English who started its construction in 1769, under the command of Lord George Montgomery, by making a parade ground and constructing barracks and kitchens to accommodate two companies of soldiers, they never got to complete the project. That was left to the French who, in 1786, finally completed the fort and named it Fort Castries. In 1789 they renamed it Fort République and in 1790, Fort Liberté.

But this situation did not last very long either, for the British retook Fort Liberté in 1793, returned it to the French in 1801, took it again in 1803 and finally kept a garrison of 600 men there until 1854, even though all the roofs had been lost in a hurricane in 1847.

Today, as Fort King George, no longer concerned with war and no longer needed for protection, it stands as a proud guardian of Tobago's past. From all aspects the view is superb. There is a commanding view of the entire sweep of Rockly Bay all the way down to Lowlands Point (where the new Tobago Hilton has recently been constructed). Over to the east Tobago's windward villages rise in the mist and sea spray and to the south the Atlantic goes its majestic way. The lighthouse contains the optical apparatus that had originally been used at Point Galera in Trinidad, now converted for electrical operation.

Only ten of the original 30 structures of the fort's complex have survived the ravages of time and weather. Among these are the officers' mess, the powder magazine, a water tank, the commander's residence, the military hospital and the prison.

On the lower level of the grounds there is a fascinating old building of coral rock and stone, surrounded by a 20-foot (60 m) stone wall and completely overshadowed by a massive samaan tree. This was probably the powder magazine. It's an eerie sort of place; only the fall of a leaf or the whistle and flutter of a bird disturbs the silence.

There are huge trees on the fort and a particular group of royal palms looking down on Rockly Bay is very striking. Cannons and piles of shot add atmosphere and the entire area is very well kept; the green grass seems to go rolling right down to the sea.

The Tobago Museum and at least one other government department are located up at the fort and to reach the fort itself you must pass through the grounds of the Scarborough Hospital.

Fort King George is truly a beautiful place, rewarding at any time of the day but particularly in the early morning or late evening. It invests each visit with new pleasure: the pleasure of its trees and shrubbery; the pleasure of its silence; the pleasure of others who come to enjoy it. The hustle and bustle of its life is finished now; the marching feet and roar of cannon are long silenced, but the grass and trees hold their secrets.

Tobago Museum

Located in the old barrack guardhouse at Fort King George, the Tobago Museum houses two floors of displays and information:

- indigenous Amerindian artefacts – pottery, weapons, tools, etc.
- colonial and military historical documents and artefacts
- historical maps, charts, paintings.
- rocks, fossils, shells
- stamps and coins
- household utility objects
- documents of colonial administration, plantation and the slave era
- a small research library.

There are over half a million pieces on display and in reserve. Assistance is given to students engaged in research, and group workshops and lectures are arranged. The curator of the museum is Mr Edward Hernandez. Opening times are Monday to Friday, 9.00 a.m.–5.00 p.m. (doors close 4.30 p.m.) The museum is closed on public holidays.

The Tobago Museum at Fort King George (MIKE TOY)

| 16 |
The Windward Road

For adventure-story enthusiasts the expression 'to windward' no doubt conjures up romantic images of sea travel in the old days – visions of four-masted ships beating up a windward coast under full sail, with white water at their bows and in their wakes. But the heyday of wind-driven ships off Tobago's shores has past, and 'going windward' today involves no more than getting into a bus, private car or taxi and travelling from Scarborough along the Windward Road which heads out east to the villages along a route that follows the Atlantic coast.

There are 18 villages along this route and most of them afford superb views of the sea and of the land as well, if you happen to be on

King's Bay on the Windward Road (MIKE TOY)

a promontory and can see along the distant coast. The villages are John Dial, Hope, Mount St George, Studley Park, Goodwood, Goldsborough, Pembroke, Glamorgan, Richmond, Belle Garden, Kendal, Argyle, Roxborough, Louis d'Or, Betsy's Hope, Delaford, Speyside and Charlotteville – names all reminiscent of the island's European settlement. This is the only Tobago coastline from which, on a clear day, depending upon your position, you can see the north coast of Trinidad. It is certainly a trip worth making. The villages are quaint and beautiful and you can do the tour on your own or using a guide, of which there are many.

John Dial is the first village you reach. Before the Claude Noel Highway was built, the Windward Road ran through Bacolet but now, with the Highway running to the north of Bacolet and bypassing it entirely, the Windward Road officially starts at John Dial. People usually ask, 'Who was John Dial?' The answer … no one really knows. A good guess is that he was the old landowner of the plantation there, but it's just a guess; he could also have been a slave named after his master. It's a small village and quickly passed through. Before you know it you're heading down into **Hope**, which has a lovely stretch of beach that is nothing if not tempting. This is Hillsborough Bay. Don't let it tempt you into the water. There are rip tides here that make this a dangerous place to swim. The villagers themselves will warn you. But it's great for contemplation, for gathering stones, shells and driftwood and examining any Atlantic debris. There's an agricultural farm at Hope and although the village is small it's very scenic and wooded up at the back.

Mount St George is larger than Hope, but much of the village lies inland; because it's hilly, you have sea views from some vantage points. From the Windward Road though, you get your first glimpses of Barbados Bay at **Studley Park**, which was earlier named Georgetown and was the first capital of Tobago until, because of the unhealthy conditions of the nearby swamp, the seat of government and all the armaments of the fort which defended it – **Fort Granby** – were moved to Scarborough, the new capital. In 1770 the first shipment of sugar made in Tobago was shipped from Barbados Bay, which is itself a rather attractive scoop of a bay on the western side of Granby Point.

Fort Granby is the second oldest fort site on the island, and was actually the first to be built by the British. It is named after the Marquis of Granby, a British military hero of the Seven Years War. All that remains is a soldier's gravestone.

Granby Point on the windward coast, the site of Fort Granby (MIKE TOY)

Granby Point juts out into the Atlantic, having Barbados Bay on one coast and Pinfold Bay on the other, both of them very historic stretches of coastline. There are benches on the point within a white picket fence and white gazebos. From here one can see the ocean currents clearly defined on the sea's surface, making their way in various directions. Of the two islands offshore, the larger, Smith's Island, is home to many gulls, boobies and pelicans and you also have a ringside view of those magnificent frigatebirds sailing up the coast to St Giles. Pinfold Bay, the scene of many a naval battle, is not a swimming area – there are too many currents and it is too deep – but fishing from the rocks in low tide is a great local pastime.

Back on the road and directly overlooking Pinfold Bay is the **First Historical Café and Bar**. There is no other Historical Café and Bar, but the owner, Kenneth Washington, just decided to establish his precedence in advance. This is a rewarding stop for a cold drink and snack, where one gains a great deal of information about Tobago through the many signs, posters and pictures decorating its internal walls that relate to every aspect of the island's history. Quite a unique approach to bartending!

181

The First Historical Café and Bar (MIKE TOY)

From **Goodwood**, the next village, there is an excellent view of misty mountains and small islands in the distance across the sea, towards Roxborough. Cedar trees grow profusely on the hillsides, interspersed with patches of vegetable and flower gardens, deep gullies and the ubiquitous breadfruit and banana trees.

Goldsborough brings you to the **Rainbow Falls** and the rather special nature trails of that part of the country. If you're interested in waterfalls and rivers, a visit to the falls can of course be arranged.

At Richmond, there is a stately old plantation home, **Richmond Great House**, which was built in the eighteenth century and rebuilt from time to time, having been occupied by the original family that owned it for about 200 years. It was badly damaged by Hurricane Flora in 1963, but has been sympathetically restored, retaining many of the beautiful aspects of the old building which convey a general air of elegance, such as wooden floors, high ceilings, large kitchen and antique furniture. It now functions as an upmarket guesthouse. The owner, a retired history professor, always welcomes visitors and invites them to look at his extensive African art collection.

Richmond Great House (MIKE TOY)

Belle Garden is best seen right after you pass it. The bay is far from the main road, but you can turn onto the bay road if you wish and take a look at **Belle Garden House**, which occupies the site of the original Great House of the Belle Garden Estate, and enjoy the superb view that is to be had from this location. There's also a good chance of seeing wildfowl in the nearby wetlands down in the beach area. When you do continue on the main road and get to the 15-mile post, stop, look back to your right and enjoy the stark rocks and steep hills of Belle Garden's coastline rising from the sea, its vegetation curiously shaped by the wind; the Atlantic here is dark blue, and dramatically turquoise and white at its edges.

Just ahead on your route, at sea level, are **Kendal** and **Argyle**, with Argyle's exciting falls and a river offering good pools for bathing.

Roxborough is a historically interesting little town, scene of the famous Belmanna Riots which are still re-enacted each year during Heritage Festival. After Emancipation, because of the shortage of local labour, Barbadian farmers were imported to live and work on the

View up the windward coast from Fort King George (MIKE TOY)

estates. Everything they needed was provided by the owners, which left them constantly in debt to these owners and not able to make a good living for themselves. Led by a woman name Mary Jane, known as Ma Tiggy, they decided to demonstrate. In the confrontation Ma Tiggy was shot by Belmanna, the chief of police, and the now-famous riot, in which Belmanna was killed, resulted.

A dramatic old silk cotton tree, hoary with mistletoe and bromeliads, stands in a small graveyard at **Betsy's Hope**. Betsy was Elizabeth, the plantation owner's daughter, whose hope of freedom for her father's slaves was never realised in her lifetime.

The plant nurseries of **Louis d'Or** are visible from the road. Tobago buys most of its fruit trees and ornamental plants here. Beyond the orchard there's a cool river with a deep pool; its grassy banks provide very good picnic grounds.

The Louis d'Or Nurseries, near Roxborough *following pages* (MIKE TOY)

LITTLE TOBAGO OR
BIRD OF PARADISE ISLAND

Little Tobago, also known as Bird of Paradise Island, is situated in the Atlantic east of Speyside and, being just about a mile and a half (2.5 km) from the mainland, is easily reached by a hired pirogue from the village. It's a star-shaped little island of approximately 248 acres, about one mile (1.5 km) long and well covered with various types of trees and bushes. It's hilly, with the highest peak being about 780 feet (145 m) above sea level. As a result the small valleys between its hills afford very good cover for the birds that live there.

There are no longer any birds of paradise on the island. In 1909, the owner of the island, Sir William Ingram, an Englishman and newspaper proprietor with cocoa estates in Trinidad, had the idea of developing a colony of greater birds of paradise (*Paradise apoda*). To this end he obtained 24 males and 24 females from Dutch New Guinea and released them on the island, adding two more females later on. Unfortunately the birds never totally thrived in this new environment and those that managed to survive were finally destroyed in the hurricane that struck Tobago in 1963. It should be noted though, that this island is the only place in the world where the bird of paradise ever existed outside its natural habitat.

Sir William died in 1924 and his widow inherited the island but did not survive him for more than a year. Their heirs, by deed drawn up on 28 May 1928, then conveyed the island and the birds to the Government and people of Trinidad and Tobago, on condition that it be kept as a bird sanctuary and that the birds of paradise be preserved.

Little Tobago continues to be an important sea-bird sanctuary in the Caribbean area even without its birds of paradise, for it is a highly accessible nesting site for the red-billed tropicbird and home to many other species of birds such as motmots, hummingbirds, gulls, boobies, sooty terns and pigeons. There are also large populations of insects such as scorpions and spiders, centipedes, lizards, hermit crabs, bats and others, making the island a veritable haven for those interested in these species.

The sanctuary is in the care of the Forestry Section of the Division of Agriculture, Forestry and Marine Affairs of the Tobago House of Assembly. This department provides and maintains the trails on the island to allow visitors easy access.

Going through **Delaford**, around a particularly sharp bend on a steep hill, you're suddenly looking down on a superb view of **King's Bay** with its hundreds of waving coconut trees stretching down to the water's edge. From here the road turns inwards to cross the mountains, through rainforest country with heavily wooded mountainsides, on its way to Speyside. There are dangerous curves but the greenery is fantastic, and in the dry season the blooming immortelles attract hordes of parrots and other birdlife.

Suddenly out of the woods, you're at the crest of a hill and below you, across an unbelievably blue sea, are Little Tobago and Goat Island and of course, Speyside itself with its quaint colourful houses on the steep hillsides. There's a lookout with benches for your relaxation at this point and fruit stalls offer refreshment.

Speyside is very scenic. There are great views of the sea, including one of the Bookends, a famous dive. **Little Tobago** and **Goat Island** are best seen from Speyside and there are many glass-bottomed boats willing to take you on a trip to these islands to snorkel and view the reef, which is thought by many to be far more beautiful than Buccoo. Snorkelling and scuba diving here are exceptional and you can also visit Little Tobago to see the magnificent frigatebirds, tropicbirds, boobies, pelicans and gulls and enjoy the drama of that spectacular scenery – sheer cliffs diving into the sea, mountains of foaming sea spray and wide-winged birds wheeling and diving in the midst of it all.

Back on the land there's **Jemma's Sea View Kitchen and Tree House Restaurant**, serving succulent lobster and shrimp dishes, **Manta Lodge** with a very good bar and **Blue Waters Inn** where you can also hire boats for your trip to the islands. There's a beautiful old water wheel at the fork of the road that leads to Blue Waters, which provided the power for the sugar plantation of long ago.

Charlotteville is only about a six-minute trip away from Speyside beyond a steep mountain road, but your reward lies at the top of Flagstaff Hill when you have your first view of that sleepy little village, clustered around the imposing **Man O' War Bay**, which incidentally has had many names bestowed upon it by various European settlers, not the least curious of which are 'Grote Kuylsack Bay', a Dutch contribution and 'Kurische Bay' from the Courlanders. The English named it John Moore's Bay after Commodore John Moore of the Royal Navy

Looking over Speyside towards Goat Island and Little Tobago *opposite* (MIKE TOY)

Water wheel and ruin at Speyside (MIKE TOY)

and finally Man O' War Bay because so many men-of-war and sailing ships used it for anchorage.

London Bridge, a popular dive location, can be seen from **Flagstaff Hill**. The hill used to be part of the Observatory Estate, a highly productive sugar estate in its day; during World War II it certainly lived up to the name of that estate, for the American armed services erected a radio tracking station here which allowed them to track the movements of German U-boats in the Caribbean.

Charlotteville, familiarly abbreviated by all to C.Ville, also offers such cosy little bays as Sand Bay, Lovers Bay and the pièce de résistance, Pirate's Bay. Fishing is good off the jetty here and the village is extremely welcoming. **Cambleton Battery** in Charlotteville is one of the numerous batteries erected around the island, which were manned by trusted slaves and local militia to protect shipping in the special bays. Cambleton was built in 1777 to afford protection from American privateers during the American War of Independence.

ROMANTIC TOBAGO

Love may make the world go round but love is not always romantic. Tobago is: blue skies, balmy breezes and shimmering turquoise and blue seas; golden poui trees flaming on the hillsides, bananaquits, blue emperor butterflies, angel fish and manta rays; smiling people, glorious summer days.

This is Tobago. Paradise on the flip side of your plane ticket. Come solo or with a friend. Tobago's romance is not only for lovers, but lovers are always welcome. You can walk into a sunset, dine to the soft tones of a steel orchestra, have breakfast under a waterfall, or baissez down to soca and calypso.

Whatever you do, Tobago adds that special touch. Given an available partner you can even decide to get married here, and Tobago is willing to help with this as well. Since 1966 the island's legislation has been changed to assist those visitors who wish to get married. The Marriage Act of 1996 permits couples to marry as quickly as three days after their arrival on the island.

Certain conditions apply, of course. Both of the involved parties must be non-residents of Trinidad and Tobago. In other words if you're a visitor marrying a local person, you can't take advantage of this special legislation – you have to follow the usual route. Visitors must be in the country for at least three days, counting from the day after the day of arrival, and must go to either the Warden's Office, Tobago or the Registrar General's Office, Tobago or Trinidad in order to declare their intention to marry and pay the required fees.

Documents such as a passport and other proofs of who you are must be presented upon application for a licence at any of these offices, and it's safe to say that although the matter can be settled in a day, it's more likely to take at least three days for the paperwork to be done.

With this simple exercise completed and the licence obtained, the wedding can take place. Where and how depends completely upon you. There have been weddings on boats out at sea, weddings under the waves in a scuba dive, under a waterfall, barefooted on the beach. The choice is yours and there are many people and organisations qualified and willing to help with all the arrangements. Many hotels and elegant restaurants offer their beautiful surroundings for wedding ceremonies.

| 17 |
Additional information

Places of interest

These are some of the most popular attractions on the island (in alphabetical order):

Adventure Farm and Nature Reserve   Arnos Vale
Argyle Waterfall   Roxborough
Arnos Vale Water Wheel   Arnos Vale
The Art Gallery   Hampden, Lowlands
Belle Garden House   Belle Garden
Bon Accord Lagoon   Bon Accord
Botanic Gardens   Scarborough
Buccoo Reef   accessible from Pigeon Point or Buccoo village

(PHOTO BY DONALD NAUSBAUM)

Cambleton Battery   Charlotteville
Crusoe's Cave   Crown Point
Cuffie River Nature Retreat   Moriah
Fine Arts Centre (being repaired)   Scarborough
Fort Granby   Studley Park
Fort James   Plymouth
Fort King George   Scarborough
Fort Milford   Crown Point
Fort Monck   Mount Irvine
Grafton Caledonia Bird and Wildlife Sanctuary   Grafton
Grave of Gang Gang Sara   Golden Lane
King's Bay
Little Tobago   Speyside
Louis d'Or Gardens   Louis d'Or
Lovers' Retreat   Plymouth
Main Ridge Forest Reserve
Man O' War Bay   Charlotteville
Mount Pleasant Anglican Church   Mount Pleasant
Mystery Tombstone   Plymouth
Providence Aqueduct   Providence
Rainbow Falls   Goldsborough
Richmond Great House   Richmond
Speyside Water Wheel   Speyside
Tobago Historical Museum   Scarborough

Hotels, guesthouses, bed and breakfast accommodation

Many hotels, guesthouses and bed and breakfast establishments on the island offer accommodation in a range of prices. Those on the following shortlist have been inspected by the Tobago House of Assembly Tourist Board.

Ann's Villa
Bacolet
Tel: 639-5200

Arnos Vale Vacation Apartments
Plymouth
Tel: 639-1362
Email: DavidSedlock@acm.org

Arthur's By the Sea
Crown Point
Tel: 639-0196
Email: arthurs@trinidad.net

Bacolet Bay Apartments
Bacolet
Tel: 639-2955

(PHOTO BY DONALD NAUSBAUM)

Blue Waters Inn
Batteaux Bay, Speyside
Tel: 660-4341
Email: bwi@bluewatersinn.com

Bougainvillaea Hotel
Studley Park
Tel: 660-2075

Conrado Beach Resort
Milford Ext. Road, Pigeon Point
Tel: 639-0145

Coral Inn Guesthouse
Crown Point
Tel: 639-0967

Country Haven Guesthouse
Speyside
Tel: 660-5901
Email: chaven99@hotmail.com

Crown Point Beach Hotel
PO Box 223, Crown Point
Tel: 639-8781
Email: crownpoint@trinidad.net

Cuffie River Nature Retreat
Runnemede Local Road,
Runnemede
Tel: 678-9020
Email: cuffiriv@tstt.net

Enchanted Waters Hotel
Shirvan Rd, Buccoo
Tel: 639-9481

Grafton Beach Resort
Black Rock
Tel: 639-0191
Email: grafton@trinidad.net

Hampden Inn
Milford Road, Hampden, Lowlands
Tel: 639-7522
Email: hampden-inn@excite.com

Hope Cottage
Calder Hall Road, Scarborough
Tel: 639-2179

Indigo Hotel
2 Horseshoe Ridge, Pleasant
Prospect, Grafton
Tel: 639-9635
Email: indigo2@tstt.net.tt

Jetway Holiday Resort
Crown Point
Tel: 639-8504

Kariwak Village Hotel
Store Bay Local Road, Crown Point
Tel: 639-8545 Email:
kariwak@tstt.net.tt

Kariwak Village Hotel (DONALD NAUSBAUM)

Hilton Hotel (DONALD NAUSBAUM)

Le Grand Courlan Resort and Spa
Black Rock
Tel: 639-9667
Email: legrand@trinidad.net

Manta Lodge
PO Box 433, Speyside
Tel: 660-5268/5030

Mills Guesthouse
Young Street, Scarborough
Tel: 639-2193

Mount Irvine Bay Hotel and Golf Club
PO Box 222, Mount Irvine
Tel: 639-8871
Email: mtirvine@tstt.net

Ocean Point
Lowlands
Tel: 639-0973

Old Donkey Cart Resort
73 Bacolet Street, Scarborough
Tel: 639-3551

Rainbow Nature Reserve
Goldsborough
Tel: 660-4755

Rex Turtle Beach Hotel
Courland Bay, Black Rock
Tel: 639-2851

Speyside Inn
189-93 Windward Road, Speyside
Tel: 660-4852
Email: yawching@trinidad.net

Surf Side Holiday Homes
Crown Point
Tel: 639-0164
Email: surfside@trinidad.net

Tobago Plantations (Hilton Hotel)
Lowlands Point
Tel: 639-8000

Viola's Place
Cor. Claude Noel Highway & Milford Road, Lowlands
Tel: 639-9441

Wood's Castle
Crown Point
Tel: 639-0803

Popular restaurants

You will find good places to eat all over the island. The following are particularly recommended:

Arnos Vale Water Wheel Restaurant and Nature Park
Arnos Vale Estate, Arnos Vale
Tel: 660-0814/0815

Best of Thymes
Crown Point
Tel: 639-0207

Black Rock Café
Black Rock
Tel: 639-7625

Blue Crab Restaurant
Robinson Street, Scarborough
Tel: 639-2737

Bonkers
Store Bay Local Road, Crown Point
Tel: 639-7173

Café Under D Mango Tree
Black Rock
Tel: 639-8964

Dillon's Seafood Restaurant
Crown Point
Tel: 639-8765

Dry Dock Restaurant and Bar
Fort Granby
Tel: 660-2537

Eleven Degrees North
Store Bay (off Pigeon Point Road)
Tel: 639-0996

Emerald Restaurant
Pleasant Prospect
Tel: 639-8272

First Historical Café and Bar
Pinfold Bay
Tel: 660-2233

Golden Star Restaurant
Crown Point
Tel: 639-0873

Indigo
Pleasant Prospect
Tel: 639-9635

Jemma's Sea View Kitchen Tree House
Speyside
Tel: 660-4066

Kariwak Village Restaurant
Kariwak Village, Store Bay Local
Road, Crown Point
Tel: 639-8442/8545

La Tartaruga Restaurant
Buccoo Village
Tel: 639-0940

Old Donkey Cart House
Bacolet
Tel: 639-6124/2357/3551

Papillon Restaurant
Mount Irvine
Tel: 639-9941

Patino's Restaurant and Bar
Shirvan Road, Buccoo
Tel: 639-9481

Petunia's Café
Milford Road, Lambeau
Tel: 639-6878

Rouselles
Bacolet
Tel: 639-4738

Seahorse Inn
Old Grafton Beach Road, Black
Rock
Tel: 639-0686

Shirvan Watermill
Shirvan Road, Mount Pleasant
Tel: 639-0000

Special beaches

There are beautiful beaches all over Tobago that you will enjoy. Those listed below are truly special ones that offer superb bathing and should not be missed. But you should let the spirit of adventure guide you as well.

- Store Bay
- Pigeon Point
- Mount Irvine Bay
- Stone Haven and Black Rock
- Grand Courland or Turtle Beach
- Castara
- Englishman's Bay
- Small Bacolet
- Canoe Bay (for children)
- Man O' War Bay, Charlotteville
- Castara Bay

Places of worship
Anointed Ministries, Main Street, Bon Accord
Church of God, Milford Road (Anglican)
Ethiopian Orthodox Church, Darrel Spring Road
Masjid, Lowlands (Muslim)
Open Bible Church, Mount Grace, Scarborough
Pentecostal Church, Smithsfield Road, Scarborough
St Andrew's Church (Anglican), Young Street, Scarborough
St Joseph's Roman Catholic Church, Bacolet Street, Scarborough
Scarborough Methodist Church, Jct. of 4th Street and Main Street, Scarborough
Seventh Day Adventist Church, Rockly Vale

Bibliography
Archibald, Douglas, *Tobago: 'Melancholy Isle', Volume 1, 1498-1771*.
Carmichael, G., *The History of the West Indian Islands of Trinidad and Tobago* (London, 1961).
Discover Trinidad and Tobago. The official publication of the Trinidad and Tobago Hotel and Tourism Association (Trinidad and Tobago). Various issues.
Eckert, Karen L., *Endangered Sea Turtles of Tobago* (with kind permission of Environment Tobago).
Elder, J. D., *Tobago's Peculiar Culture* (mimeograph).
ffrench, Richard, *A Guide to the Birds of Trinidad and Tobago*, second edition (New York, 1991).
Hill, Errol, *The Trinidad Carnival: Mandate for a National Theatre* (Austin, Texas, 1972).
Laurence, K. O., *Tobago in Wartime 1793-1815* (Barbados, 1995).
Ottley, C. R., *The Complete History of the Island of Tobago in the West Indies* (Trinidad, 1949).
Tobago House of Assembly, *Tenth Anniversary Brochure 1980-1990* (Trinidad and Tobago, 1990).
Tobago Today. The informative news magazine for the visitor to Tobago (Trinidad and Tobago). Various issues.